DIVER'S HANDBOOK OF UNDERWATER CALCULATIONS

Diver working at 200 fsw. Courtesy: Union Carbide Corporation, Linde Division.

DIVER'S HANDBOOK OF UNDERWATER CALCULATIONS

Wayne C. Tucker

Cornell Maritime Press
Centreville, Maryland

Front cover photo courtesy Union Carbide Corporation, Linde Division; back cover photo courtesy J. S. Brower & Associates, Inc. (BROCO).

Library of Congress Cataloging in Publication Data

Tucker, Wayne C   1947-
   Diver's handbook of underwater calculations.
   Bibliography: p.
   Includes index.
    1. Diving, Submarine—Handbooks, manuals, etc.
I. Title.
VM981.T82   627'.72   79-27451
ISBN 0-87033-254-6

Manufactured in the United States of America
First edition, 1980; fourth printing, 1994

Dedicated to
my friend, Ross Johnson,
lost at sea, September, 1976.

ACKNOWLEDGEMENTS

I wish to express my sincere thanks to George Tucker, Frances Tucker, and Elizabeth Tucker for their support during the time I wrote this book. I wish to extend my gratitude to Lieutenant Commander William Bacon and Commander Karl M. Duff of the United States Navy Sea Systems Command for their technical assistance and the information they provided.

Many thanks also to Bruce Basset, H.N. Schenck, Frank White and John McAniff for their assistance, to Cyn Kuhn who did the art work, and finally to Helps Secretarial Service for typing the manuscript.

TABLE OF CONTENTS

FOREWORD

Between diver and engineer lies a sea of useful information which has never been deciphered. This book presents some of that information although many books could evolve from the void between scientists and practitioners. Since my life's work has been a fortunate combination of education and commercial diving experience, I have endeavored to present the practical insights born of this combination of ocean engineering and commercial diving.

As a practical matter, then, the information presented here provides the diver, engineer, or supervisor with a means to obtain the data needed to do his job; as well as an explanation of each subject in clear yet not oversimplified language. The reader should be advised that conversion factors used throughout the text are from Table 1-1 in Chapter 1.

Where it becomes impractical to present equations and solutions because of complexity, tables are provided from mathematical analysis or current information. Some values have never been actually measured. Unmeasured values derived from mathematical analysis are given as "approximate" values to provide the reader with an idea of what to expect—an educated guess.

Where accuracy is required, as in computing air supply, the equations are developed from fundamentals and carefully explained at each step. Examples are worked through to show how to apply the equations to the real problems encountered in commercial diving.

Diving operations require all who are involved to be able to determine: What size? How many? How much time? I hope this book will help the user to answer many of these questions.

CHAPTER 1: MEASUREMENT

The foundation of any discussion regarding calculations is measurement. The units of measurement most commonly used in commercial diving are the English units. However, the metric system is now in the process of implementation; therefore, the conversion from English units to metric units is of tremendous importance to the working diver. It is up to each individual to learn the metric system and how to use it. This chapter will discuss the units of measurement in both systems and will deal with the problem of conversion from one system to the other as it relates to diving. The diver equipped to handle either system will be riding the new wave of change rather than swept away by it.

SOME BASIC PRINCIPLES

The English system of measurement is based on units which were commonly used as convenient measuring devices such as the *foot* being a measure of distance. The division of the foot into twelve inches and the inch into halves, quarters, eighths, and so on necessitates lengthy arithmetic manipulation. Conversion of inches into feet, yards into miles, requires conversion factors which are cumbersome to deal with and hard to remember.

The great advantage of the metric system is that all units of measure are multiples or submultiples of 10. When converting units of measurement within the metric system, you need only move a decimal point. The more complex calculations involving units of measurement such as pressure can be converted by powers of 10 rather than having to change feet into square inches (multiply by 144) and ounces into pounds (divide by 16).

The problem with the metric system is that it is unfamiliar to most people. Most have a "feeling" for inches, feet and yards. It is difficult to estimate in meters or kilometers without practice. To express a measurement in metrics to someone unfamiliar with it is also a problem. If you say the temperature is 20° Celsius, most people have no idea whether that is hot or cold. The metric system is like learning a new language—it takes a while to be able to "think metric." However, doing calculations with metrics is another matter. You need only convert all of your measurements from English units to metric units by simple conversion factors (Table 1-1), and your calculations become greatly simplified. The final answer can be converted back to the English system if desired. In this way you can learn the metric system and get a feeling for it while you simplify your calculations. Typical prefixes and their numerical equivalents are:

$\dfrac{1}{1{,}000{,}000}$	$\dfrac{1}{1{,}000}$	$\dfrac{1}{100}$	$\dfrac{1}{10}$	Quantity	1,000	1,000,000
micro-	milli-	centi-	deci-	meter gram	kilo-	mega-
10^{-6}	10^{-3}	10^{-2}	10^{-1}	1	10^{3}	10^{6}

DISTANCE AND SIZE

Apparent distance and size underwater are affected by the magnification effect of air and water (Fig. 1-1). The mediums of air and water between the diver's eyes and the object of vision give a magnification effect due to the different densities of air and water (Snell's law). Distance appears shorter than it actualy is and objects appear larger than they really are. The factor of magnification is 4/3 underwater. For this reason, any important distance or size underwater should be measured with an appropriate tool.

Photography is affected underwater by the magnification effect. The focal distance set on the camera must be adjusted to compensate for the magnification effect. Therefore, the distance from the object to the camera must be 4/3

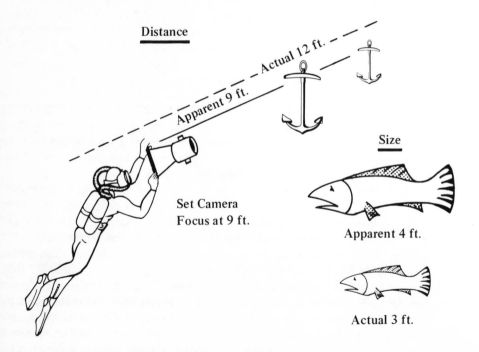

Fig. 1-1. Apparent vs. actual size and distance underwater: Apparent size is due to magnification of air-water interface.

the focal distance set on the camera. For example, if the camera focus is set at 3 feet, the distance from the camera to the object must be (4/3), (3 feet) = (4 feet).

The unit measure of distance in the metric system is the meter. One-hundredth of a meter is called a centimeter. One-thousandth of a meter is called a millimeter. One thousand meters equal one kilometer. The meter corresponds roughly to the yard:

$$1 \text{ yard} = 0.9144 \text{ meter}$$
$$1 \text{ inch} = 2.54 \text{ centimeters}$$
$$1/16 \text{ inch} = 1.59 \text{ millimeters}$$
$$1 \text{ meter} = 3.28 \text{ feet}$$
$$1 \text{ centimeter} = .394 \text{ inches}$$
$$1 \text{ millimeter} = .0394 \text{ inches}$$

To convert distance to metrics simply multiply by the appropriate conversion factor given in Table 1-1.

Example 1-1:

The Nikonus camera has focus adjustments given in feet and meters. You have measured the distance from an anchor you wish to photograph at 2 yards. What must your focus be set at on your camera? Give the answer in feet and meters.

Answer:

Two yards actual distance underwater will be an apparent or focus distance of (2 yards) (3 feet per yard) (3/4) = 4.5 feet. To convert feet into meters multiply by .3048 (Table 1.1). (4.5 feet) (.3048 meters per foot) = 1.37 meters.

Example 1-2:

You survey a sunken yacht and record the following for a partial salvage plan:

LOCATION OF WRECK: 2 miles south of Fisher Island

DEPTH TO TOP OF WRECK: 35 feet

DEPTH TO BOTTOM: 45 feet

LOA (Length Over All): 60 feet

ONE HOLE AFT OF ENGINE ROOM, PORT SIDE: 1 foot, 6 inches high by 2 feet, 7 inches long

HULL THICKNESS: 7/8 inch wood planks

BOTTOM CURRENT AT MAXIMUM TIDE: 1 1/2 knots

The salvage master is a Frenchman and wants your survey in metrics.

Answer:

LOCATION OF WRECK: (2 miles) (1.609 kilometers per mile) = 3.22 kilometers south of Fisher Island

DEPTH TO TOP OF WRECK: (35 feet) (.3048 meters per foot) = 10.67 meters

DEPTH TO BOTTOM: (45) (.3048 meters per foot) = 13.72 meters
LOA: (60 feet) (.3048 meters per foot) = 18.3 meters
ONE HOLE AFT OF ENGINE ROOM, PORT SIDE: (18 inches) (2.54 centimeters per inch) = 45.72 centimeters high; (31 inches) (2.54 centimeters per inch) = 78.74 centimeters long
HULL THICKNESS: (.875 inches) (25.4 millimeters per inch) = 22.2 millimeters thick
BOTTOM CURRENT AT MAXIMUM TIDE: (1.5 knot) (1.8432 [kilometers per hour] per knot) = 2.78 kilometers per hour

WEIGHT

Underwater, weight is affected by buoyancy (Archimedes' principle). The effect of buoyancy on the diver will be discussed in detail in Chapters 3 and 6. Here we will discuss measurement of weight as it relates to diving and the conversion of English weight to metric weight.

Weight is determined by the density of an object times the volume of that object. It is important for the diver to understand weight in terms of density and volume because the weight of an object in air will differ from its weight in water. How greatly it differs will depend upon the density of the object. For example, lead is of sufficient density so that its weight is not affected significantly underwater. Aluminum, on the other hand will lose about 38% of its weight underwater. The human body will lose virtually 100% of its weight underwater because the density of the human body is nearly the same as water. Objects such as styrofoam if submerged will have a lifting capacity due to the fact that they are less dense than water.

We measure weight in the English system in ounces, pounds, and tons. The metric units of weight are grams, kilograms, and metric tons.

$$1 \text{ ounce} = 28.35 \text{ grams}$$
$$1 \text{ pound} = .45 \text{ kilograms}$$
$$1 \text{ ton} = .9078 \text{ metric ton}$$

Example 1-3:
You have a 25-pound weight belt and a 40-pound weight belt. How many grams does your 25-pound weight belt weigh? How many kilograms does your 40-pound weight belt weigh?

Answer:
(25 pounds) (454 grams per pound) = 11,350 grams
(40 pounds) (.454 kilograms per pound) = 18.6 kilograms

Example 1-4:
The deck winch on your lifting rig is rated at 10 tons maximum lift capacity. The salvage master has calculated he needs a 9.0 metric ton lift to break the ground force and raise the wreck. Can you do it?

Answer:

(9.0 metric tons) (1.10 tons per metric ton) = 9.9 tons

Just barely

TEMPERATURE

Temperature is normally recorded in degrees Fahrenheit or degrees Celsius. Temperatures in scientific calculations are converted to degrees Rankine from Fahrenheit in the English system and to degrees Kelvin from degrees Celsius in the metric system. The Rankine scale and the Kelvin scale are called *Absolute Temperature* scales. Zero degrees on the Absolute Temperature scale marks Absolute Zero, where theoretically all molecular motion stops.

The single most common error in gas laws calculations (Chapter 2) is neglecting to convert temperatures to the Absolute Temperature scale.

To convert temperatures from degrees Fahrenheit to Absolute Temperature add 460° (Absolute Temperature with the English system called degrees Rankine):

$$°R = °F + 460$$

To convert temperatures from degrees Celsius to Absolute Temperature, add 273° (Absolute Temperature with the metric system called degrees Kelvin):

$$°K = °C + 273$$

To convert Fahrenheit to Celsius

$$°C = 5/9 \, (°F - 32)$$

To convert Celsius to Fahrenheit

$$°F = 9/5 \, (°C + 17.8)$$

Example 1-5:

The water temperature is recorded at 68°F. Give the temperature on the metric absolute scale (°K):

Answer:

$$
\begin{aligned}
°K &= °C + 273 \\
°C &= 5/9 \, (°F - 32) \\
°K &= 5/9 \, (°F - 32) + 273 \\
&= 5/9 \, (68 - 32) + 273 \\
&= 5/9 \, (36) + 273 \\
&= 293°K
\end{aligned}
$$

PRESSURE

Pressure is defined as a force per unit area. Generally, it is expressed in pounds per square inch (psi). In metric units it is expressed in grams per square centimeter or kilograms per square meter. A useful measure of pressure for many underwater calculations is expressed in atmospheres. Absolute pressure and gauge pressure are in use for many calculations and will also be discussed.

Pressure in atmospheres is derived from atmospheric pressure at sea level which is 14.7 pounds per square inch. One atmosphere of pressure is 14.7 psi. Approximately every 33 additional feet of sea water depth adds this same pressure and is therefore equivalent to 1 atmosphere of pressure. Underwater, the absolute pressure in atmospheres is found by the relationship:

$$P = \frac{D + 33}{33}$$

where
P = Absolute pressure in atmospheres
D = Depth of water in feet

Absolute pressure includes the atmospheric pressure. Gauge pressure does not include the pressure of the atmosphere and is therefore zero at sea level.

$$P_{gauge} = P_{absolute} - P_{atmosphere}$$

$$P_{gauge} = \frac{D}{33}$$

Example 1-6:
Your pressure gauge records your scuba tank pressure at 1,500 psi. What is the absolute pressure in your tank?
Answer:

$$P_{absolute} = P_{gauge} + P_{atmosphere}$$

$$= 1,500\,psi + 14.7\,psi$$
$$= 1,514.7\,psi$$

Example 1-7:
Your are going to dive to 50 meters. What will be the absolute pressure in atmospheres? What will be the absolute pressure in kgm/m^2? What will be your decompression schedule if bottom time equals 20 minutes?

Answer:

$$P = \frac{D + 33}{33}$$

$$D = (50 \text{ meters}) (3.28 \text{ feet per meter})$$
$$= 164 \text{ feet}$$

$$P = \frac{164 + 33}{33}$$

$$= 5.97 \text{ atmospheres}$$

or converting D to meters

$$P = \frac{D + 33 (.3048)}{33 (.3048)}$$

$$= \frac{D + 10.06}{10.06}$$

where
P = Pressure in atmospheres
D = Depth in meters

then

$$P = \frac{50 + 10.06}{10.06}$$

$$= 5.97 \text{ atmospheres}$$

Pressure of 1 atmosphere is 14.7 psi

$$(5.97 \text{ atmospheres}) \left(\frac{14.7 \text{ pounds per square inch}}{\text{atmosphere}}\right)$$

$$= 87.75 \text{ psi}$$

Converting psi to kilograms per square meter

$$(87.76 \text{ psi}) (.4536 \text{ kg/lb}) (1.55 \times 10^3 \frac{\text{in}^2}{\text{m}^2}) = 6.17 \times 10^4 \text{ kg/m}^2$$

Decompression schedule for 50 meter dive, (Bottom Time) = 20 min (from Navy Air Decompression Tables use 170-foot table).

BT = 20 min
Time to first stop = 2:30 min
Decompression stops: 20 ft = 4 min; 10 ft = 15 min
Total ascent time 21:50, including 20 seconds to surface after first stop

SUMMARY OF RELATIONS AND EQUATIONS

Size, Distance

Optical magnification underwater—4/3 actual size
For camera, set focus at 3/4 actual distance

Temperature

$$°F = 9/5(°C + 17.8)$$
$$°C = 5/9(°F - 32)$$
$$°R \text{ (English Absolute temperature)} = °F + 460$$
$$°K \text{ (metric absolute temperature)} = °C + 273$$

Pressure

Absolute pressure in atmospheres

$$P = \frac{D + 33}{33}$$

where D = depth in feet

$$P = \frac{D + 10.06}{10.06}$$

where D = depth in meters

Gauge pressure

$$P_{gauge} = P_{absolute} - P_{atmosphere}$$

$$= \frac{D}{33}$$

where D = depth in feet

$$= \frac{D}{10.06}$$

where D = depth in meters

Table 1-1 Conversion Factors

To convert	Into	Multiply by	To convert	Into	Multiple by
acres	sq feet	43,560.0		gram-cal/sec	0.0700
	sq meters	4,047.0		horsepower	3.929×10^{-4}
	sq miles	1.562×10^{-3}		watts	0.2931
	sq yards	4,840.0	Btu/min	foot-lbs/sec	12.96
atmospheres	cms of mercury	76.0		horsepower	0.02356
	ft of water (at 04°C)	33.90		kilowatts	0.01757
	in of mercury (at 0°C)	29.92		watts	17.57
	kgs/sq cm	1.0333	Btu/sq ft/min	watts/sq in	0.1221
	kgs/sq meter	10,332.0	bushels	cu ft	1.2445
	pounds/sq in	14.70		cu in	2,150.4
	tons/sq ft	1.058		cu meters	0.03524
barrels (oil)	gallons (oil)	42.0		liters	35.24
bars	atmospheres	0.9869		pecks	4.0
	dynes/sq cm	10^6		pints (dry)	64.0
	kgs/sq meter	1.020×10^4		quarts (dry)	32.0
bars	pounds/sq ft	2,089.0	Centigrade	Fahrenheit	(C° x 9/5) + 32
	pounds/sq in	14.50	centigrams	grams	0.01
Btu	ergs	1.0550×10^{10}	centiliters	liters	0.01
	foot-lbs	778.3	centimeters	feet	3.28×10^{-2}
	gram-calories	252.0		inches	0.3937
	horsepower-hrs	3.931×10^{-4}		kilometers	10^{-5}
	joules	1,054.8		meters	0.01
	kilogram-calories	0.2520		miles	6.214×10^{-6}
	kilogram-meters	107.5		millimeters	10.0
	kilowatt-hrs	2.928×10^{-4}		mils	393.7
Btu/hr	foot-pounds/sec	0.2162		yards	1.094×10^{-2}

Table 1-1 Conversion Factors
(Continued)

To convert	Into	Multiply by	To convert	Into	Multiply by
centimeter-dynes	cm-gram	1.020×10^{-3}	cubic centimeters	gallons (U.S. liq)	2.642×10^{-4}
	meter-kgs	1.020×10^{-8}		liters	0.001
	pound-feet	7.376×10^{-8}		pints (U.S. liq)	2.113×10^{-3}
centimeter-grams	cm-dynes	980.7		quarts (U.S. liq)	1.057×10^{-3}
	meter-kgs	10^{-5}	cubic feet	bushels (dry)	0.8036
	pound-feet	7.233×10^{-5}		cu cms	28,320.0
centimeters of	atmospheres	0.01316		cu inches	1,728.0
mercury	feet of water	0.4461		cu meters	0.02832
	kgs/sq meter	136.0		cu yards	0.03704
	pounds/sq ft	27.85		gallons (U.S. liq)	7.48052
	pounds/sq in	0.1934		liters	28.32
centimeters/sec	feet/min	1.9685		pints (U.S. liq)	59.84
	feet/sec	0.03281		quarts (U.S. liq)	29.92
	kilometers/hr	0.036	cubic feet/min	cu cms/sec	472.0
	knots	0.01943		gallons/sec	0.1247
	meters/min	0.6		liters/sec	0.4720
	miles/hr	0.02237		pounds of water/min	62.43
	miles/min	3.728×10^{-4}	cubic feet/sec	million gals/day	0.646317
centimeters/sec/	feet/sec/sec	0.03281		gallons/min	448.831
sec	kms/hr/sec	0.036	cubic inches	cu cms	16.39
	meters/sec/sec	0.01		cu feet	5.787×10^{-4}
	miles/hr/sec	0.02237		cu meters	1.639×10^{-5}
cubic centimeters	cu feet	3.531×10^{-5}		cu yards	2.143×10^{-5}
	cu inches	0.06102		gallons (U.S. liq)	4.329×10^{-3}
	cu meters	10^{-6}		liters	0.01639
	cu yards	1.308×10^{-6}		mil-feet	1.061×10^{5}

To convert	Into	Multiple by
cubic meters	pints (U.S. liq)	0.03463
	quarts (U.S. liq)	0.01732
	bushels (dry)	28.38
	cu cms	10^6
	cu feet	35.31
	cu inches	61,023.0
	cu yards	1.308
	gallons (U.S. liq)	264.2
	liters	1,000.0
	pints (U.S. liq)	2,113.0
	quarts (U.S. liq)	1,057.0
cubic yards	cu cms	7.646×10^5
	cu ft	27.0
	cu inches	46,656.0
	cu meters	0.7646
	gallons (U.S. liq)	202.0
	liters	764.0
	pints (U.S. liq)	1,615.9
	quarts (U.S. liq)	807.9
cubic yards/min	cubic ft/sec	0.45
	gallons/sec	3.367
	liters/sec	12.74
days	hours	24.0
	minutes	1,440.0
	seconds	86,400.0
deciliters	liters	0.1

To convert	Into	Multiple by
decimeters	meters	0.1
degrees (angle)	minutes	60.0
	radians	0.01745
	seconds	3,600.0
degrees (terr great circle)	miles (naut)	60.0
degrees/sec	radians/sec	0.01745
	revolutions/min	0.1667
	revolutions/sec	2.778×10^{-3}
dekagrams	grams	10.0
dekaliters	liters	10.0
dekameters	meters	10.0
drams	grams	1.7718
	grains	27.3437
	ounces	0.0625
dynes	grams	1.020×10^{-3}
	joules/cm	10^{-7}
	joules/meter (newtons)	10^{-5}
	kilograms	1.020×10^{-6}
	poundals	7.233×10^{-5}
	pounds	2.248×10^{-6}
dynes/sq cm	bars	10^{-6}
ergs	Btu	9.480×10^{-11}
	dyne-centimeters	1.0
	foot-pounds	7.367×10^{-8}

Table 1-1 Conversion Factors
(Continued)

To convert	Into	Multiple by
	gram-calories	0.2389×10^{-7}
	grams-cms	1.020×10^{-3}
	horsepower-hrs	3.7250×10^{-14}
	joules	10^{-7}
	kg-calories	2.389×10^{-11}
	kg-meters	1.020×10^{-8}
	kilowatt-hrs	0.2778×10^{-13}
	watt-hours	0.2778×10^{-10}
ergs/sec	Btu/min	$5,688.0 \times 10^{-9}$
	ft-lbs/min	4.427×10^{-6}
	ft-lbs/sec	7.3756×10^{-8}
	horsepower	1.341×10^{-10}
	kg-calories/min	1.433×10^{-9}
	kilowatts	10^{-10}
fathoms	feet	6.0
feet	centimeters	30.48
	kilometers	3.048×10^{-4}
	meters	0.3048
	miles (naut)	1.645×10^{-4}
	miles (stat)	1.894×10^{-4}
	millimeters	304.8
	mils	1.2×10^{4}
feet of water	atmospheres	0.02950
	in of mercury	0.8826
	kgs/sq cm	0.03048
	kgs/sq meter	304.8

To convert	Into	Multiple by
	pounds/sq ft	62.43
	pounds/sq in	0.4335
feet/min	cms/sec	0.5080
	feet/sec	0.01667
	kms/hr	0.01829
	meters/min	0.3048
	miles/hr	0.01136
feet/sec	cms/sec	30.48
	kms/hr	1.097
	knots	0.5921
	meters/min	18.29
	miles/hr	0.6818
	miles/min	0.01136
feet/sec/sec	cms/sec/sec	30.48
	kms/hr/sec	1.097
	meters/sec/sec	0.3048
	miles/hr/sec	0.6818
foot-pounds	Btu	1.286×10^{-3}
	ergs	1.356×10^{7}
	grams-calories	0.3238
	hp-hrs	5.050×10^{-7}
	joules	1.356
	kg-calories	3.24×10^{-4}
	kg-meters	0.1383
	kilowatt-hrs	3.766×10^{-7}
foot-pounds/min	Btu/min	1.286×10^{-3}

To convert	Into	Multiply by
	foot-pounds/sec	0.01667
	horsepower	3.030×10^{-5}
	kg-calories/min	3.24×10^{-4}
	kilowatts	2.260×10^{-5}
foot-pounds/sec	Btu/hr	4.6263
	Btu/min	0.07717
	horsepower	1.818×10^{-3}
	kg-calories/min	0.01945
	kilowatts	1.356×10^{-3}
furlongs	rods	40.0
	feet	660.0
gallons	cu cms	3,785.0
	cu feet	0.1337
	cu inches	231.0
	cu meters	3.785×10^{-3}
	cu yards	4.951×10^{-3}
	liters	3.785
	pints	8.0
	quarts	4.0
gallons (liq. Br. Imp)	gallons (U.S. liq)	1.20095
gallons (U.S.)	gallons (Imp)	0.83267
horsepower (metric) (542.5 ft lb/sec)	horsepower (9550 ft lb/sec)	0.9863
horsepower (550 ft lb/sec)	horsepower (metric) (542.5 ft lb/sec)	1.014

To convert	Into	Multiply by
horsepower	kg-calories/min	10.68
	kilowatts	0.7457
	watts	745.7
horsepower (boiler)	Btu/hr	33.479
	kilowatts	9.803
horsepower-hrs	Btu	2,547.0
	ergs	2.6845×10^{13}
	foot-lbs	1.98×10^{6}
	gram-calories	641,190.0
	joules	2.684×10^{6}
	kg-calories	641.1
	kg-meters	2.737×10^{5}
	kilowatt-hrs	0.7457
hours	days	4.167×10^{-2}
	minutes	60.0
	seconds	3,600.0
	weeks	5.952×10^{-3}
inches	centimeters	2.540
	feet	8.333×10^{-2}
	meters	2.540×10^{-2}
	miles	1.578×10^{-5}
	millimeters	25.40
	mils	1,000.0
	yards	2.778×10^{-2}
inches of mercury	atmospheres	0.03342
	feet of water	1.133

Table 1-1 Conversion Factors
(Continued)

To convert	Into	Multiple by
inches of water (at 4°C)	kgs/sq cm	0.03453
	kgs/sq meter	345.3
	pounds/sq ft	70.3
	pounds/sq in	0.4912
	atmospheres	2.458×10^{-3}
	inches of mercury	0.07355
	kgs/sq cm	2.540×10^{-3}
	ounces/sq in	0.5781
	pounds/sq ft	5.204
	pounds/sq in	0.03613
joules	Btu	9.480×10^{-4}
	ergs	10^7
	foot-pounds	0.7376
	kg-calories	2.389×10^{-4}
	kg-meters	0.1020
	watt-hrs	2.778×10^{-4}
joules/cm	grams	1.020×10^4
	dynes	10^7
	joules-meter (newtons)	100.0
	poundals	723.3
	pounds	22.48
kilograms	dynes	980,665.0
	grams	1,000.0
	joules/cm	0.09807
	joules/meter (newtons)	9.807
	poundals	70.93
	pounds	2.205
	tons (long)	9.842×10^{-4}
	tons (short)	1.102×10^{-3}
kilograms/cu meter	grams/cu cm	0.001
	pounds/cu ft	0.06243
	pounds/cu in	3.613×10^{-5}
	pounds/mil-foot	3.405×10^{-10}
kilograms/meter	pounds/mil-foot	0.6720
kilograms/sq cm	atmospheres	0.9678
	feet of water	32.81
	inches of mercury	28.96
	pounds/sq ft	2,048.0
	pounds/sq in	14.22
kilograms/sq meter	atmospheres	9.678×10^{-5}
	bars	98.07×10^{-6}
	feet of water	3.281×10^{-3}
	inches of mercury	2.896×10^{-3}
	pounds/sq ft	0.2048
	pounds/sq in	1.422×10^{-3}
kilograms/sq mm	kgs/sq meter	10^6
kilograms-calories	Btu	3.968
	foot-pounds	3,088.0
	hp-hrs	1.560×10^{-3}

To convert	Into	Multiply by
	joules	4,186.0
	kg-meters	426.9
	kilojoules	4.186
	kilowatt-hrs	1.163×10^{-3}
kilogram meters	Btu	9.294×10^{-3}
	ergs	9.804×10^{7}
	foot-pounds	7.233
	joules	9.804
	kg-calories	2.342×10^{-3}
	kilowatt-hrs	2.723×10^{-6}
kiloliters	liters	1,000.0
kilometers	centimeters	10^{5}
	feet	3,281.0
	inches	3.937×10^{4}
	meters	1,000.0
	miles	0.6214
	millimeters	10^{6}
	yards	1,094.0
kilometers/hr	cms/sec	27.78
	feet/min	54.68
	feet/sec	0.9113
	knots	0.5396
	meters/min	16.67
	miles/hr	0.6214
kilometers/hr/sec	cms/sec/sec	27.78
	ft/sec/sec	0.9113

To convert	Into	Multiply by
	meters/sec/sec	0.2778
	miles/hr/sec	0.6214
kilowatts	Btu/min	56.92
	foot-lbs/min	4.426×10^{4}
	foot-lbs/sec	737.6
	horsepower	1.341
	kg-calories/min	14.34
	watts	1,000.0
kilowatt-hrs	Btu	3,413.0
	ergs	3.600×10^{13}
	foot-lbs	2.655×10^{6}
	gram-calories	859,850.0
	horsepower-hrs	1.341
	joules	3.6×10^{6}
	kg-calories	859.85
	kg-meters	3.671×10^{5}
knots	feet/hr	6,080.2
	kilometers/hr	1.8532
	nautical miles/hr	1.0
	statute miles/hr	1.1516
	yards/hr	2,027.0
	feet/sec	1.689
league (marine)	miles (naut)	3.0
liters	bushels (U.S. dry)	0.02838
	cu cm	1,000.0

Table 1-1 Conversion Factors
(Continued)

To convert	Into	Multiple by	To convert	Into	Multiple by
	cu feet	0.03531		feet/sec	3.281
liters	cu inches	61.02		kilometers/hr	3.6
	cu meters	0.001		kilometers/min	0.06
	cu yards	1.308×10^{-3}		miles/hr	2.237
	gallons (U.S. liq)	0.2642		miles/min	0.03728
	pints (U.S. liq)	2.113	meters/sec/sec	cms/sec/sec	100.0
	quarts (U.S. liq)	1.057		ft/sec/sec	3.281
liters/min	cu ft/sec	5.886×10^{-4}		kms/hr/sec	3.6
	gals/sec	4.403×10^{-3}		miles/hr/sec	2.237
lumens/sq ft	foot-candles	1.0	meter-kilograms	cm-dynes	9.807×10^{7}
lux	foot-candles	0.0929		cm-grams	10^{5}
meters	centimeters	100.0		pound-feet	7.233
	feet	3.281	micrograms	grams	10^{-6}
	inches	39.37	microliters	liters	10^{-6}
	kilometers	0.001	miles (naut)	degrees (terr great circle)	0.016666
	miles (naut)	5.396×10^{-4}		feet	6,080.20
	miles (stat)	6.214×10^{-4}		kilometers	1.853248
	millimeters	1,000.0		meters	1,853.248
	yards	1.094		miles (statute)	1.1516
meters/min	cms/sec	1.667		yards	2,025.4
	feet/min	3.281	miles (statute)	centimeters	1.609×10^{5}
	feet/sec	0.05468		feet	5,280.0
	kms/hr	0.06		inches	6.336×10^{4}
	knots	0.03238		kilometers	1.609
	miles/hr	0.03728		meters	1,609.0
meters/sec	feet/min	196.8			

To convert	Into	Multiply by
miles/hr	miles (naut)	0.8684
	yards	1,760.0
	cms/sec	44.70
	feet/min	88.0
	feet/sec	1.467
	kms/hr	1.609
	kms/min	0.02682
	knots	0.8684
	meters/min	26.82
	miles/min	0.01667
miles/hr/sec	cms/sec/sec	44.70
	feet/sec/sec	1.467
	kms/hr/sec	1.609
	meter/sec/sec	0.4470
miles/min	cms/sec	2,682.0
	feet/sec	88.0
	kms/min	1.609
	miles (naut)/min	0.8684
	miles/hr	60.0
mil-feet	cu inches	9.425×10^{-6}
milliers	kilograms	1,000.0
milligrams	grams	0.001
milligrams/liter	parts/million	1.0
milliliters	liters	0.001
millimeters	centimeters	0.1
	feet	3.281×10^{-3}
	inches	0.03937
	kilometers	10^{-6}
	meters	0.001
	miles	6.214×10^{-7}
	mils	39.37
	yards	1.094×10^{-3}
million gals/day	cu ft/sec	1.54723
mils	centimeters	2.540×10^{-3}
	feet	8.333×10^{-5}
	inches	0.001
	kilometers	2.540×10^{-8}
	yards	2.778×10^{-5}
miner's inches	cu ft/min	1.5
minutes (angles)	degrees	0.01667
	quadrants	1.852×10^{-4}
	radians	2.909×10^{-4}
	seconds	60.0
myriagrams	kilograms	10.0
myriameters	kilograms	10.0
ounces	grams	16.0
	grains	437.5
	grams	28.349527
	pounds	0.0625
	ounces (troy)	0.9115
	tons (long)	2.790×10^{-5}
	tons (metric)	2.835×10^{-5}

Table 1-1 Conversion Factors
(Continued)

To convert	Into	Multiple by	To convert	Into	Multiple by
ounces (fluid)	cu inches	1.805	pounds	joules/cm	1.383×10^{-3}
	liters	0.02957		joules/meter (newtons)	0.1383
ounces (troy)	grains	480.0		kilograms	0.01410
	grams	31.103481		pounds	0.03108
	ounces (avdp)	1.09714		drams	256.0
	pennyweights (troy)	20.0		dynes	44.4823×10^4
	pounds (troy)	0.08333		grains	7,000.0
ounces/sq in	pounds/sq in	0.0625		grams	453.5924
parts/million	grains/U.S. gal	0.0584		joules cm	0.04448
	grains/Imp gal	0.07016		joules/meter (newtons)	4.448
	pounds/million gal	8.345	pounds (troy)	kilograms	0.4536
pennyweights (troy)	grains	24.0		ounces	16.0
	ounces (troy)	0.05		ounces (troy)	14.5833
	grams	1.55517		poundals	32.17
	pounds (troy)	4.1667×10^{-3}		pounds (troy)	1.21528
pints (dry)	cu inches	33.60		tons (short)	0.0005
pints (liq)	cu cms	473.2		grains	5,760.0
	cu feet	0.01671		grams	373.24177
	cu inches	28.87		ounces (avdp)	13.1657
	cu meters	4.732×10^{-4}		ounces (troy)	12.0
	cu yards	6.189×10^{-4}		pennyweights (troy)	240.0
	gallons	0.125		pounds (avdp)	0.822857
	liters	0.4732		tons (long)	3.6735×10^{-4}
	quarts (liq)	0.5		tons (metric)	3.7324×10^{-4}
poundals	dynes	13,826.0			
	grams	14.10			

18

To convert	Into	Multiple by	To convert	Into	Multiple by
pounds of water	tons (short)	4.1143×10^{-4}		inches of mercury	2.036
	cu feet	0.01602		kgs/sq meter	703.1
	cu inches	27.68		pounds/sq ft	144.0
	gallons	0.1198	quadrants (angle)	degrees	90.0
pounds of water/min	cu-ft/sec	2.670×10^{-4}		minutes	5,400.0
pound-feet	cm-dynes	1.356×10^{7}		radians	1.571
	cm-grams	13,825.0		seconds	3.24×10^{5}
	meter-kgs	0.1383	quarts (dry)	cu inches	67.20
pounds/cu ft	grams/cu cm	0.01602	quarts (liq)	cu cms	946.4
	kgs/cu meter	16.02		cu feet	0.03342
	pounds/cu in	5.787×10^{-4}		cu inches	57.75
	pounds/mil-foot	5.456×10^{-9}		cu meters	9.464×10^{-4}
pounds/cu in	gms/cu cm	27.68		cu yards	1.238×10^{-4}
	kgs/cu meter	2.768×10^{4}		gallons	0.25
	pounds/cu ft	1,728.0		liters	0.9463
	pounds/mil-foot	9.425×10^{-6}	radians	degrees	57.30
pounds/ft	kgs/meter	1.488		minutes	3,438.0
pounds/in	gms/cm	178.6		quadrants	0.6366
pounds/mil-foot	gms/cu cm	2.306×10^{6}		seconds	2.063×10^{5}
pounds/sq ft	atmospheres	4.725×10^{-4}	radians/sec	degrees/sec	57.30
	feet of water	0.01602		revolutions/min	9.549
	inches of mercury	0.01414		revolutions/sec	0.1592
	kgs/sq meter	4.882	radians/sec	revs/min/min	573.0
	pounds/sq in	6.944×10^{-3}	radians/sec/sec	revs/min/sec	9.549
pounds/sq in	atmospheres	0.06804		revs/sec/sec	0.1592
	feet of water	2.307	revolutions	degrees	360.0

Table 1-1 Conversion Factors
(Continued)

To convert	Into	Multiple by
revolutions/min	quadrants	4.0
	radians	6.283
	degrees/sec	6.0
	radians/sec	0.1047
	revs/sec	0.01667
revolutions/min/min	radians/sec/sec	1.745×10^{-3}
	revs/min/sec	0.01667
	revs/sec/sec	2.778×10^{-4}
revolutions/sec	degrees/sec	360.0
	radians/sec	6.283
	revs/min	60.0
revolutions/sec/sec	radians/sec/sec	6.283
	revs/min/min	3,600.0
	revs/min/sec	60.0
rods	feet	16.5
seconds (angle)	degrees	2.778×10^{-4}
	minutes	0.01667
	quadrants	3.087×10^{-6}
	radians	4.848×10^{-6}
square centimeters	circular mils	1.973×10^{5}
	sq feet	1.076×10^{-3}
	sq inches	0.1550
	sq meters	0.0001
	sq miles	3.861×10^{-11}
	sq millimeters	100.0
	sq yards	1.196×10^{-4}
square feet	acres	2.296×10^{-5}
	circular mils	1.833×10^{8}
	sq cms	929.0
	sq inches	144.0
	sq meters	0.09290
	sq miles	3.587×10^{-8}
	sq millimeters	9.290×10^{4}
	sq yards	0.1111
square inches	circular mils	1.273×10^{6}
	sq cms	6.452
	sq feet	6.944×10^{-3}
	sq millimeters	645.2
	sq mils	10^{6}
	sq yards	7.716×10^{-4}
square kilometers	acres	247.1
	sq cms	10^{10}
	sq ft	10.76×10^{6}
	sq inches	1.550×10^{9}
	sq meters	10^{6}
	sq miles	0.3861
	sq yards	1.196×10^{6}
square meters	acres	2.471×10^{-4}
	sq cms	10^{4}
	sq feet	10.76
	sq inches	1,550.0
	sq miles	3.861×10^{-7}

To convert	Into	Multiply by
	sq millimeters	10^6
	sq yards	1.196
square miles	acres	640.0
	sq feet	27.88×10^6
	sq kms	2.590
	sq meters	2.590×10^6
	sq yards	3.098×10^6
square millimeters	circular mils	1,973.0
	sq cms	0.01
	sq feet	1.076×10^{-5}
	sq inches	1.550×10^{-3}
square mils	circular mils	1.273
	sq cms	6.452×10^{-6}
	sq inches	10^{-6}
square yards	acres	2.066×10^{-4}
	sq cms	8,361.0
	sq feet	9.0
	sq inches	1,296.0
	sq meters	0.8361
	sq miles	3.228×10^{-7}
	sq millimeters	8.361×10^5
temperature (°C) + 273	absolute temperature (°C)	1.0
temperature (°C) + 17.78	temperature (°F)	1.8

To convert	Into	Multiple by
temperature (°F) + 460	absolute temperature (°F)	1.0
temperature (°F) − 32	temperature (°C)	5/9
tons (long)	kilograms	1,016.0
	pounds	2,240.0
	tons (short)	1.120
tons (metric)	kilograms	1,000.0
	pounds	2,205.0
tons (short)	kilograms	907.1848
	ounces	32,000.0
	ounces (troy)	29,166.66
	pounds	2,000.0
	pounds (troy)	2,430.56
	tons (long)	0.89287
	tons (metric)	0.9087
tons (short)/sq ft	kgs/sq meter	9,765.0
	pounds/sq in	2,000.0
tons of water/24 hours	pounds of water/24 hours	83.333
	gallons/min	0.16643
	cu ft/hr	1.3349
watts	Btu/hr	3.413
	Btu/min	0.05688

Table 1-1 Conversion Factors
(Continued)

To convert	Into	Multiple by	To convert	Into	Multiple by
	ergs/sec	10^7		horsepower-hrs	1.341×10^{-3}
	foot-lbs/min	44.27		kilogram-calories	0.8598
	foot-lbs/sec	0.7378		kilograms-meters	367.2
	horsepower	1.341×10^{-3}		kilowatt-hrs	0.001
	horsepower (metric)	1.360×10^{-3}	yards	centimeters	91.44
	kg-calories/min	0.01433		feet	3.0
	kilowatts	0.001		kilometers	9.144×10^{-4}
watt-hours	Btu	3.413		meters	0.9144
	ergs	3.60×10^{10}		miles (naut)	4.934×10^{-4}
	foot-pounds	2,656.0		miles (stat)	5.682×10^{-4}
	gram-calories	859.85		millimeters	914.4

CHAPTER 2: PRESSURE, VOLUME, AND TEMPERATURE RELATIONSHIPS

PRESSURE AT DEPTH CALCULATIONS

If one cubic foot of seawater were weighed on a scale, the weight would read 64.043 pounds. The weight that seawater exerts on an object underwater equals 64.043 pounds for every cubic foot of water above it. Pressure is generally expressed in pounds per square inch (psi). Therefore every foot of water depth exerts a pressure of

$$\frac{64.043 \text{ lb/ft}^3}{144 \frac{\text{in}^2}{\text{ft}^2}} = .445 \text{ psi/ft}$$

and the absolute pressure at any depth in pounds per square inch is given by

$$P_{absolute} = P_{gauge} + P_{atmosphere}$$
$$P = (.445)(D) + 14.7 \qquad \textbf{[2.1]}$$

where
P = pressure in pounds per square inch
D = depth of seawater in feet

For metric calculation we convert Equation 2-1 using Table 1-1.

$$.445 \text{ psi/ft} = (.445 \frac{\text{lbs.}}{\text{sq in-ft}})(453.6 \frac{\text{grams}}{\text{lb}})(.1533 \frac{\text{sq in}}{\text{sq cm}})(3.28 \frac{\text{ft}}{\text{m}})$$

$$= 101.5 \frac{\text{grams}}{\text{cm}^2\text{-meter}}$$

$$P = 101.5 (D) + (14.7 \text{ psi})(453.6 \frac{\text{grams}}{\text{lb}})(.1533 \frac{\text{sq in}}{\text{sq cm}})$$
$$P = 101.5 (D) + 1022.2 \qquad \textbf{[2.2]}$$

where
P = pressure in grams per square centimeter
D = depth in meters

Example 2-1:
What is the gauge pressure at a depth of 10 meters?
Give answer in:
a. grams/cm^2
b. psi
c. atmospheres

Answer:

a. $P_{gauge} = P_{absolute} - P_{atmosphere}$

$\quad P_g = (101.5)(D)$

$ = (101.5)(10)$

$ = 1015 \text{ grams/cm}^2$

b. $10 \text{ meters} = (10m)\,(3.28\,\frac{ft}{m})$

$ = 32.8 \text{ ft}$

$\quad P_{gauge} = (.445)\,(D)$

$\phantom{b.\quad P_{gauge}} = (.445)\,(32.8)$

$\phantom{b.\quad P_{gauge}} = 14.6 \text{ psi}$

c. $1 \text{ atmosphere} = 14.7 \text{ psi}$

$$P_g = \frac{14.6 \text{ psi}}{14.7 \text{ psi}}$$

$ = .993 \text{ atmospheres}$

Notice that:

$$1 \text{ atmosphere} = 14.7 \text{ psi}$$
$$= 33 \text{ ft of seawater}$$
$$= 10.06 \text{ meters of seawater}$$

Example 2-2:

A ping-pong ball is submerged to a depth of 25 feet where it collapses.

a. What was the absolute pressure at that depth?

b. If the surface area of the ball was 4 square inches, how many absolute pounds of force were on the outside of the ball?

c. What was the net force on the surface of the ball if the internal pressure of the ball was 5 psig?

Answer:

a. $P = (.445)\,(D) + 14.7$

$ = (.445)(25) + 14.7$

$ = 25.825 \text{ psia}$

b. Force $= (\text{Pressure})\,(\text{Area})$

$ = (25.825 \text{ psi})\,(4 \text{ square inches})$

$ = 103.3 \text{ pounds}$

c. $P_{absolute\ internal} = P_{gauge} + P_{atm}$

$ = 5 \text{ psi} + 14.7 \text{ psi}$

$ = 19.7 \text{ psia}$

$\quad P_{net} = P_{outside} - P_{inside}$

$\phantom{c.\quad P_{net}} = 25.825 \text{ psi} - 19.7 \text{ psi}$

$\phantom{c.\quad P_{net}} = 6.125 \text{ psi}$

 Net Force $= (\text{Net Pressure})\,(\text{Area})$

$ = (6.125 \text{ psi})\,(4 \text{ in}^2)$

$ = 24.5 \text{ pounds}$

Example 2-3:

A scientist gives you an expensive instrument encased in a water-tight plexiglass box. He says the box can take a pressure of 50 pounds per square inch. The pressure inside the case is 1 atmosphere absolute. How deep can you dive with this instrument?

Answer:

P_{gauge} not to exceed 50 psi

50 psi = (.445) (D)

D = 112.36 feet

Note:

If you asked the scientist what the pressure inside the case was and he said there was no pressure at all; you would have to clarify whether he meant there was zero pressure (a vacuum) or whether there was just atmospheric pressure. If there was zero pressure in the case (a vacuum), you would be starting the dive with 14.7 psi on the outside of the case already at the surface. Your calculation would then be:

$$50\,psi - 14.7\,psi = (.445)D$$
$$D = 79.33\,feet$$

A troublesome problem arises when using cameras and other watertight cases in conjunction with a habitat or lockout system. Since the case is assembled at 1 atmosphere on the surface, it is difficult or impossible to disassemble the case inside the pressurized lockout or habitat. It may, there-fore, be necessary to send the camera to the surface to change film. If the camera can be disassembled and reassembled inside the habitat, another problem arises on excursion dives to shallower depths. The pressure inside the case may burst an o ring seal or weak part of the case (such as the film advance window) because of the lowering of pressure outside the case on ascent. The result may be ruined film or often a ruined lens.

PRESSURE-VOLUME RELATIONSHIPS

One of the most useful relationships for underwater calculations is Boyle's law. The consequence of pressure exerted on a gas produces profound effects due to the underwater environment. All divers are aware of the reduction of air supply with depth and the dangers of gas expansion on ascent. For the working diver, the effects of pressure on gas volume have many more applications. Later chapters will deal with buoyancy and lifting considerations, compressor sizes, air supply and air tools.

Figure 2-1 shows the relationship of pressure and gas volume underwater. Notice that the greatest volume change occurs in the first 33 feet of depth. Boyle's law states:

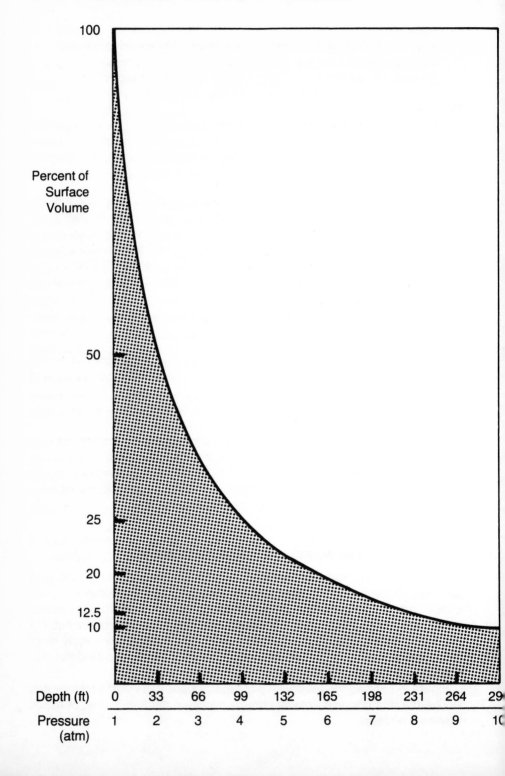

If the temperature is kept constant, the volume of a gas will vary inversely as the absolute pressure while the density will vary directly as the pressure.

$$P_1V_1 = P_2V_2$$ **[2.3]**

$$T = \text{constant}$$

The fact that gas volume doubles on ascent between 33 feet and the surface is of great importance to the diver, especially during decompression (Chapter 4). Any gas in the diver's system during ascent will expand the greatest amount and *at the fastest rate* even if the ascent rate of the diver remains constant.

The transition from 33 feet to the surface, therefore, requires successively longer and longer decompression stops because of the faster *rate* at which gas will expand. The closer the diver comes to the surface, the more time is required to allow the gas to come out of his system because of the relatively faster rate at which the pressure drops. As an example, a 1 cubic foot parcel of air ascending from a depth of 297 feet will not double in volume until it reaches 132 feet (traveling a distance of 165 feet). But it will double in volume again from 132 feet to 50 feet (traveling half the distance) and it will double again from 50 feet to 8 feet (traveling only a quarter of the original distance). The total volume expansion of 1 cubic foot of air ascending from 297 feet to the surface will be 10 cubic feet, 5 of which occur from 33 feet to the surface.

Air embolism is also most likely to occur during the last 33 feet of ascent to the surface because of the rapid volume change rate. Any air in the diver's lungs will expand more rapidly from 33 feet to the surface than at greater depths even though the diver's ascent rate is constant.

When air is used to lift objects from the bottom, the last 33 feet of ascent will make or break the lifting operation. The air expansion will cause pressure in a rigid container or expansion of a flexible container. An expanding container will accelerate as it rises and may burst. A rigid container with no pressure relief value may burst also. The most likely place for this trouble to occur is during the last 33 feet of ascent to the surface.

Gas law calculations are done using *absolute* pressures and temperature. If we compute pressure in atmospheres underwater, Equation 2.3 becomes:

$$\left(\frac{D_1 + 33}{33}\right)V_1 = \left(\frac{D_2 + 33}{33}\right)V_2$$ **[2.4]**

Fig. 2-1. Gas volume vs. pressure underwater.

At the surface, $D_1 = 0$ and our equation is simplified:

$$V_1 = (\frac{D + 33}{33}) V_2 \qquad\qquad \text{[2.5]}$$

D in feet

$$V_1 = (\frac{D + 10.06}{10.06}) V_2$$

$$\text{[2.6]}$$

D in meters

Example 2-4:

At the surface, you inflate your life vest 40 cubic inches to compensate for some tools you are carrying. When you dive to 150 feet, how much air will be left in your vest?

Answer:

$$V_1 = \frac{(D + 33)}{33} V_2$$

$$40 = (\frac{150 + 33}{33}) V_2$$

$$V_2 = 7.2 \text{ cu in}$$

Example 2-5:

What will be the gas volume change ascending from 30 meters to 10 meters?

Answer:

$$(\frac{D_1 + 10.06}{10.06}) V_1 = (\frac{D_2 + 10.06}{10.06}) V_2$$

$$(\frac{30 + 10.06}{10.06}) V_1 = (\frac{10 + 10.06}{10.06}) V_2$$

$$3.98 V_1 = 1.99 V_2$$

$$V_2 = 1.996 V_1$$

Volume will almost double

PRESSURE AND TEMPERATURE RELATIONSHIPS

For constant volume problems pressure and temperature are directly variable. Generally, the only significant problem this presents to the diver is pressure drop in scuba tanks upon cooling. Temperature also affects pressure in air lines; and pressure affects temperature and humidity in decompression chambers and habitats. Air lines, chambers and habitats, however, are not steady state problems. They involve compressible fluid flow, friction, and gas-vapor mixtures. These situations require complex thermodynamic and fluid dynamic equations for which iterative matharnatical methods are needed to compute values. These mathematical methods are beyond the scope of this book, but we will discuss the problems of gas pressure and temperature qualitatively for understanding and in order to give some rule of thumb methods as well as tables of values for general use in later chapters. For the present problem we use the relationship:

$$P_2 = \frac{P_1 T_2}{T_1}$$

[2.7]

$$V = constant$$

Example 2-6:
  Your scuba tank is filled to 2500 psi, but the temperature of the tank rises to 180°F during filling. When you hit the water, which is 45°F, what will be your tank pressure?

Answer:

$$P_2 = \frac{P_1 T_2}{T_1}$$

$$P_2 = \frac{(2500\,psi)\,(45 + 460)}{(180 + 460)}$$

$$= 1,973\,psi$$

VOLUME AND TEMPERATURE RELATIONSHIPS

  Charles' law states: *If the pressure of a gas is kept constant, the volume of gas will vary directly as the absolute temperature*. The relationship of volume and temperature is shown, together with one example for understanding.

$$V_2 = \frac{V_1 T_2}{T_1}$$

[2.8]

$$P = constant$$

Example 2-7:
  On the beach an inner tube is inflated to 3 cubic feet of air at 90°F. When you take the tube into 50°F water, how much volume will you lose? (Assume constant pressure.)

Answer:

$$V_2 = \frac{V_1 T_2}{T_1}$$

$$= \frac{(3\,ft^3)\,(50 + 460)}{(90 + 460)}$$

$$= 2.78\,ft^3$$

$$V_1 - V_2 = .22\,ft^3\,loss$$

PRESSURE, VOLUME AND TEMPERATURE RELATIONSHIPS

The general gas law combines Equations 2.3, 2.7, and 2.8 into one equation which can be used for all P,V,T computations. If one variable is held constant, then the general gas law reduces to one of the prior forms. The general gas law equation is:

$$\frac{P_1 V_1}{T_1} = \frac{P_2 V_2}{T_2}$$

[2.9]

Example 2-8:

At a depth of 99 feet, you inflate an airlift bag to 2 cubic feet of air. The bag has a pressure relief value set to blow at 10 psig. The temperature of the water at 99 feet is 35°F. At 75 feet is a thermocline where the temperature instantaneously rises to 60°F. If the bag can expand another cubic foot with no rise in pressure, when will the relief value blow?

Answer:

This problem presents four possibilities:

1. The pressure drop from 99 feet to 75 feet might be sufficient to expand the bag to 3 cubic feet then blow the value. (Fig. 2-2).
2. If not, when the bag reaches 75 feet the temperature rise may be sufficient to blow the valve. (Fig. 2-3).
3. Somewhere after 75 feet, the valve will blow. (Fig. 2-4 and 2-5).
4. There will not be sufficient pressure increase under these circumstances to blow the valve.

Let us first examine what occurs between 99 feet and 75 feet (Fig. 2-2). The temperature is constant and the bag can expand 1 cubic foot with no rise in pressure. The general gas law:

$$\frac{P_1 V_1}{T_1} = \frac{P_2 V_2}{T_2}$$

reduces to

$$P_1 V_1 = P_2 V_2$$

$T = $ constant

where

$$P_1 = \frac{D_1 + 33}{33} = \left(\frac{99 + 33}{33}\right) = 4 \text{ atm}$$

$$P_2 = \frac{D_2 + 33}{33} = \frac{75 + 33}{33} = 3.3 \text{ atm}$$

$$V_1 = 2 \text{ ft}^3$$

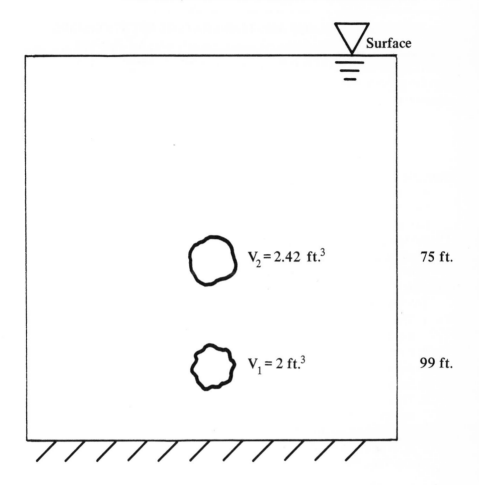

Fig. 2-2. Expansion of bag during ascent from 99 ft to 75 ft.

therefore,

$$V_2 = \frac{P_1 V_1}{P_2}$$
$$= \frac{(4)(2 \text{ ft}^3)}{3.3}$$
$$= 2.42 \text{ ft}_3$$

The bag does not rise in pressure by ascending to 75 feet because the volume is still under the 3 cubic foot maximum. We therefore analyze what happens to the bag during the temperature rise (Fig. 2-3). We assume an instantaneous change in temperature at 75 feet

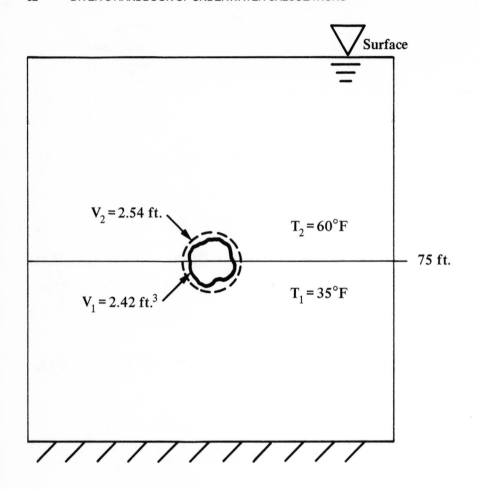

Fig. 2-3. Expansion of bag due to temperature rise at 75 ft.

so the bag does not ascend while we analyze the temperature effect. The pressure will remain constant unless the bag volume exceeds 3 cubic feet due to the temperature change. Therefore, the general gas law reduces to

$$\frac{V_1}{T_1} = \frac{V_2}{T_2}$$

$$V_2 = \frac{V_1 T_2}{T_1}$$

$$P = \text{constant}$$

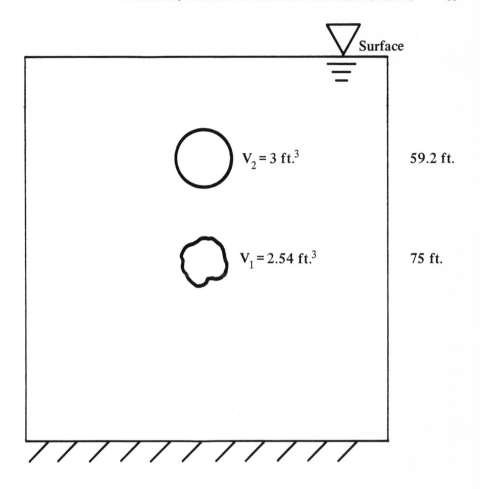

Fig. 2-4. At 59.2 ft bag reaches full volume.

where

$$V_1 = 2.42 \text{ ft}^3$$
$$T_1 = (35 + 460)$$
$$T_2 = (60 + 460)$$
$$V_2 = \frac{(2.42)\,(520)}{495}$$
$$= 2.54 \text{ ft}^3$$

The airlift bag has increased in volume through our first two possibilities but there has been no pressure increase inside the bag because of the allowable expansion of 1 cubic foot. Our third possibil-

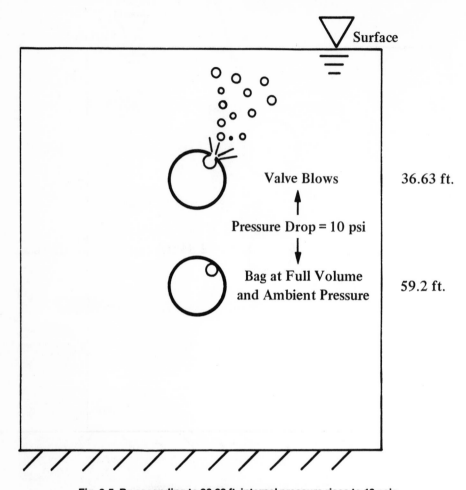

Fig. 2-5. By ascending to 36.63 ft, internal pressure rises to 10 psig.

ity allows us to expand the volume by another .46 ft³ with no rise in pressure. Let us determine at what depth the bag will reach this limit (Fig. 2-4).

$$\frac{P_1 V_1}{T_1} = \frac{P_2 V_2}{T_2}$$

From 75 feet to the surface we have a constant temperature, therefore:

$$P_1 V_1 = P_2 V_2$$

$$T = \text{constant}$$

On board the barge *Michigan*, which is laying a 10-foot diameter discharge pipe, the diver prepares to descend into Lake Michigan near Muskegon to check bedding stone. In front of him are cables suspending a section of pipe over the side. The diver is equipped with a Kirby-Morgan Superlite B-8 helmet and mounted on his back is a "bail-out" air system in case the primary system fails. A tender assists in preparations.

We are looking for the depth at which $V_2 = 3 \text{ ft}^3$.

$$P_2 = \frac{P_1 V_1}{V_2}$$

where

$$P_1 = \frac{75 + 33}{33} = 3.3 \text{ atm}$$
$$V_1 = 2.54 \text{ ft}^3$$
$$V_2 = 3 \text{ ft}^3$$

therefore

$$P_2 = \frac{(3.3)\,(2.54)}{3}$$

$$= 2.79 \text{ atm}$$
$$\frac{D_2 + 33}{33} = 2.79 \text{ atm}$$
$$D_2 = 59.2 \text{ ft.}$$

After 59.2 ft the airbag will no longer expand. Therefore, the volume will remain constant and the pressure inside the bag will rise as the pressure drops on the outside of the bag during ascent. The temperature is constant also and our equation:

$$\frac{P_1 V_1}{T_1} = \frac{P_2 V_2}{V_2}$$

reduces to

$$P_1 - P_2 = P_f$$
$$P_f = \text{final or valve pressure}$$

where

$$P_1 = \frac{(59.2 + 33)}{33} = 2.79 \text{ atm}$$

$$P_f = \frac{(10 \text{ psi})}{(14.7 \text{ psi/atm})} = .68 \text{ atm}$$

$$P_2 = \frac{D + 33}{33}$$

solving for D:

$$2.79 - \frac{(D + 33)}{33} = .68$$

$$D = (2.79 - .68) \, 33 - 33$$
$$D = 36.63 \text{ ft}$$

At 36.63 ft the pressure valve will blow.

GAS MIXING—PARTIAL PRESSURES

Dalton's law states: *The total pressure exerted by a mixture of gases is the sum of the pressures that would be exerted by each of these gases if it alone were present and occupied the total volume.*

$$P_T = P_1 + P_2 + \ldots + P_n \qquad \qquad \text{[2.10]}$$

Atmospheric air is composed of approximately 20% oxygen and 80% nitrogen. The total pressure exerted by these two gases at sea level is 14.7 psi. Oxygen therefore exerts 20% of the pressure of atmospheric air. The partial pressure of oxygen in the atmosphere is 20% of 14.7 psi or 3 psi at sea level according to Dalton's law. Nitrogen exerts the remaining 11.7 psi to make up the total.

The diver breathes air at elevated total pressures as he descends. To account for the increase in total pressure, the partial pressures of the component gases in the breathing mixture must increase. The increase in total pressure means the diver is breathing higher *concentrations* of the component gases; but the proportions of the mixture are the same. These higher concentrations cause problems for the diver.

Oxygen, the life sustaining element of the air we normally breathe, becomes poison in high concentration. It has been determined that a concentration of oxygen in a breathing mixture exceeding a partial pressure of 29.4 psi or 2 atmospheres may cause oxygen poisoning. As the diver descends, the partial pressure of the oxygen in his breathing mixture increases. Compressed air with 20% oxygen content will have a partial pressure at any depth of 20% of the absolute pressure at that depth;

$$P_{0_2} = (0.2) \, \frac{(D + 33)}{33} \qquad \qquad \text{[2.11]}$$

where
P_{0_2} = partial pressure of oxygen in atmosphere in standard air mix

D = depth in feet

or

$$P_{O_2} = (0.2)(.445D + 14.7)$$ [2.12]

where

P_{O_2} = partial pressure of oxygen in psi in standard air mix

D = depth in feet

Example 2-9:

What is the depth limit of compressed air diving if the oxygen concentration in the breathing mix is not to exceed 2 atmospheres? (Assume air = 80% nitrogen, 20% oxygen)

$$P_{O_2} = (0.2)\frac{(D + 33)}{33}$$

$$2 \text{ atm} = (0.2)\frac{(D + 33)}{33}$$

$$D = 297 \text{ feet}$$

Nitrogen, the largest component of atmospheric air, is not used by the body when breathed. At sea level, nitrogen merely flows in and out of the lungs with every breath. As the diver descends, however, the elevated partial pressure of nitrogen in his breathing medium activates another fundamental gas law.

Henry's law states: *The amount of gas that will dissolve in a liquid at a given temperature is almost directly proportional to the partial pressure of that gas.*

According to Henry's law, nitrogen dissolves in the blood and tissues of the diver's body as he descends. (Oxygen is metabolized by the body and is of no consequence in this regard). Nitrogen problems result for two reasons: (1) high concentrations of nitrogen become narcotic and impair the diver's ability to function rationally (nitrogen narcosis); (2) nitrogen dissolves in the blood and must be eliminated by the body upon ascending without allowing bubble formation in the blood and tissues (decompression sickness). Problems encountered by nitrogen elimination will be discussed in detail in Chapter 4.

Carbon dioxide is produced by the diver when he exhales and is present to a small extent in the normal atmosphere. Carbon dioxide partial pressure in the diver's breathing mixture has established tolerance levels which will be examined in Chapter 5.

Contaminants in general are present in our atmosphere. If a small concentration of contamination is allowed to enter the diver's breathing medium, it will be magnified as the diver descends. Established air quality standards and filtration systems are in effect to insure that the diver receives air purity of a high enough standard so that concentrations of contaminants do not reach dangerous levels caused by elevated pressures.

The partial pressure of any gas at any depth in psi is found by:

$$P_p = C\,(.445(D) + 14.7)$$

where
P_p = partial pressure in psi of any gas
C   = percent of gas present in mix
D   = depth

SUMMARY OF RELATIONS AND EQUATIONS

Absolute Pressure at Any Depth

$$P = (.445)\,(D) + 14.7$$

where
P = pressure in psi
D = depth in feet

$$P = (101.5)(D) + 1022.2$$

where
P = pressure in gm/cm^2
D = depth in meters

Pressure-Volume Relationships

$$P_1 V_1 = P_2 V_2$$

T = constant

$$\left(\frac{D_1 + 33}{33}\right) V_1 = \left(\frac{D_2 + 33}{33}\right) V_2$$

$$V_1 = \frac{(D + 33)}{33} V_2$$

V_1 at surface

Pressure-Temperature Relationships

$$P_2 = \frac{P_1 T_2}{T_1}$$

V = constant

Volume-Temperature Relationships

$$V_2 = \frac{V_1 T_2}{T_1}$$

P = constant

Pressure Volume-Temperature Relationships

$$\frac{P_1 V_1}{T_1} \quad \frac{P_2 V_2}{T_2}$$

Gas Mixing Partial Pressures

$$P_{Total} = P_1 + P_2 \ldots + P_n$$

Partial Pressure of any Gas at Depth

$$P_p = C(.445(D) + 14.7)$$

where

P_p = partial pressure of any gas in psi

C   = percent of gas in mixture

D   = depth in feet

CHAPTER 3: FRESH WATER VS. SEAWATER CALCULATIONS

So far, all calculations have been based on seawater as a diving medium. Due to different depth pressures, as well as altered buoyancy problems, fresh water diving presents some questions regarding decompression procedures. Since fresh water is closer in composition to pure water, one might ask why seawater was chosen as a basis for diving calculations in the first place. One obvious reason is that, due to the abundance of seawater, most of the diving is done in the ocean; but it also follows that if bottom depth errors are made in fresh water, these errors are in the diver's favor for decompression schedules. The reverse would be true in seawater if the decompression tables were based on fresh-water depth pressures. The decompression stop depths, however, must be given close attention in fresh water because of the possibility of error which would not be in the diver's favor and could cause decompression complications. These complications will be examined and discussed in detail. It might be added that most of the differences between fresh water and seawater calculations are small; but small errors can add up to serious mistakes! So let us examine and evaluate carefully the difference between fresh water and seawater with respect to diving calculations. We shall also investigate other situations which may alter our basic assumptions, such as concentrated chemical solutions, very salty water, and pollution.

BUOYANCY (See also Chapter 6)

The most obvious difference between seawater and fresh water diving is the altered buoyancy the diver experiences. If the diver was neutral in seawater, he sinks in fresh water. The volume of water the diver displaces is the same in either case, but the weight of the water he displaces in seawater is more than the weight of the same volume of fresh water (seawater is heavier because of dissolved salts). According to Archimedes' principle, the submerged diver is buoyed upward by a force equal to the weight of the water he displaces. Therefore, the diver is more buoyant in seawater and requires more lead weight to overcome the buoyancy of his diving dress than he would in fresh water.

The lifting capacity of air in fresh water is reduced because a cubic foot of fresh water weighs less than a cubic foot of seawater. When a cubic foot of air displaces a cubic foot of water, it can lift virtually the weight of the water it displaces (air weight is negligible). For lifting jobs utilizing air, a larger volume of air is required to lift an object in fresh water for two reasons; first, the object will weigh slightly more in fresh water than it would in seawater. Second, the same volume of air in fresh water will lift less weight than it would in seawater.

The weight of a submerged object is found by subtracting the weight of the volume of water the object displaces from its air weight. Fresh water weighs 62.366 pounds per cubic foot. Seawater weighs 64.043 pounds per cubic foot. The weight of an object submerged in water then becomes:

$$W_{sub} = W_{air} - W_w$$

where
W_{sub} = submerged weight of object
W_{air} = weight of object in air
W_w = weight of water displaced by object

Since weight can be expressed in terms of density and volume, we substitute the known values of density. For seawater this becomes

$$W_{sub/sea} = W_{air} - (64.043)V_{obj} \qquad \text{[3.1]}$$

where
$W_{sub/sea}$ = submerged weight of object in seawater in pounds

W_{air} = weight of object in air in pounds

W_{obj} = volume of object in cubic feet

For fresh water

$$W_{sub/fresh} = W_{air} - (62.366)V_{obj} \qquad \text{[3.2]}$$

where
$W_{sub/fresh}$ = submerged weight of object in fresh water in pounds

W_{air} = weight of object in air in pounds

V_{obj} = volume of object in cubic feet

By comparing Equations 3.1 and 3.2, it can be seen that an object submerged in fresh water will lose less of its air weight to the buoyant force of the water than it would in seawater. The object is therefore slightly heavier in fresh water. For very dense materials the difference will be miniscule. For example, lead will only gain about 4 pounds per ton in fresh water. On the other hand, concrete will gain about 50 pounds per ton under fresh water. The 50 pound weight gain coupled with the loss of lifting capacity with air amounts to about 100 pounds per ton in fresh water for concrete. This adds up to a possible error of 5% if seawater values are used to compute buoyancy of concrete in fresh water.

Example 3-1:
Two concrete cylinders 4 feet in diameter and 50 feet long are submerged. One cylinder is a navigational hazard in the ocean. The

After inspection of the one hundred year-old Georgiaville Dam in Smithfield, Rhode Island, the author works on restoring the structure. New gates will be put in place and a foundation built underwater for installation of a trash screen.

other must be removed from a fresh water lake. Calculate the submerged weight of each cylinder. Assume concrete has a density of 150 pounds per cubic foot.

Answer:

$$\text{Weight} = (\text{Density})(\text{Volume})$$
$$W = \rho V$$

$$\text{Submerged weight} = \text{air weight minus buoyant force}$$
$$W_{sub} = \rho_c V_c - \rho_w V_c$$
$$= V_c(\rho_c - \rho_w)$$

where

V_c = volume of concrete = $\pi r^2 L$

ρ_c = density of concrete 150 lb/ft^3

ρ_w = density of water: 62.366 lb/ft^3, fresh; 64.043 lb/ft^3, salt

$$W_{submerged/fresh} = \pi(4)(50)(150\text{-}62.366)$$
$$= (628.3)(87.634)$$
$$= 55,060 \text{ lbs}$$
$$W_{sub/sea} = 628.3(150\text{-}64.043)$$
$$= 54,007 \text{ lbs}$$

The cylinder under fresh water weighs nearly one-half ton more than the same cylinder under seawater. To calculate the amount of air required to lift an object underwater (disregarding container weight and drag forces, See Chapter 6), a volume of air will virtually lift the weight of the water it displaces because air weighs almost zero compared to the weight of an equal volume of water. Therefore:

$$\text{L.C.} = V_a \rho_w$$

where

L.C. = lifting capacity of air in pounds disregarding container weight and drag forces.

V_a = volume of air

ρ_w = density of water

For fresh water

$$\text{L.C.} = V_a (62.366) \tag{3.3}$$

where

L.C. = lifting capacity in pounds

V_a = volume of air in cubic feet

For seawater

$$\text{L.C.} = V_a (64.043) \qquad [3.4]$$

where
L.C. = lifting capacity in pounds
V_a = volume of air in cubic feet

Example 3-2:
Disregarding container weight and drag forces, calculate the volume of air required to lift each cylinder in Example 3-1.
Answer:

$$\text{L.C.} = \rho_w V_a$$

For seawater

$$\text{L.C.} = 54{,}007 \text{ lbs}$$
$$\rho_w = 64.043 \text{ lbs/ft}^3$$
$$54{,}007 = (64.043)(V_a)$$
$$V_a = 843 \text{ ft}^3$$

For fresh water

$$\text{L.C.} = 55{,}060 \text{ lbs.}$$
$$\rho_w = 62.366 \text{ lbs/ft}^3$$
$$55{,}060 = 62.366 (V_a)$$
$$V_a = 883 \text{ ft}^3$$

The difference of 40 cubic feet of air required between fresh water and seawater lifting capacity amounts to one and one-quarter tons possible error in calculating lifting requirements for fresh water if seawater values were used in this example.

PRESSURE

Because an equal volume of fresh water weighs less than seawater, the pressure fresh water exerts at any depth will be less than the pressure exerted at the same depth of seawater. We have established the relationship [2.1]

$$P_s = (.445)D_s + 14.7$$

for pressure in psi at any depth D_s of seawater. The relationship for fresh water is found from the density of fresh water

$$\frac{62.366 \text{ lbs/ft}^3}{144 \text{ in}^2 \text{ ft}^2} = .433 \text{ psi/ft}$$
$$P_f = (.433)D_f + 14.7 \qquad [3.5]$$

where

P_f = pressure under fresh water in psi

D_f = depth of fresh water in feet

Table 3.1 shows the gauge pressure in psi with depth for seawater and fresh water. Table 3.2 gives the pressure equivalent depths of fresh water and

Table 3-1 Gauge Pressure for Depths of Seawater and Fresh Water

Depth in Feet	Gauge Pressure in psi	
	Fresh Water	Seawater
10	4.33	4.45
20	8.66	8.9
30	12.99	13.35
40	17.32	17.8
50	21.65	22.25
60	25.98	26.7
70	30.31	31.15
80	34.64	35.6
90	38.97	40.05
100	43.3	44.5
110	47.63	48.95
120	51.96	53.4
130	56.29	57.85
140	60.62	62.3
150	64.95	66.75
160	69.28	71.2
170	73.61	75.65
180	77.94	80.1
190	82.27	84.55
200	86.6	89.0
210	90.93	93.45
220	95.26	97.9
230	99.59	102.35
240	103.92	106.8
250	108.25	111.25
260	112.58	115.7
270	116.91	120.15
280	121.24	124.6
290	125.57	129.05
300	129.9	133.5

Table 3-2 Equivalent Depths of Seawater and Fresh Water

Depth (Feet of Seawater)	Pressure Equivalent Depth (Feet of Fresh Water)
10	10.3
20	20.6
30	30.9
40	41.2
50	51.5
60	61.8
70	72.1
80	82.4
90	92.7
100	103.0
110	113.3
120	123.6
130	133.9
140	144.2
150	154.5
160	164.8
170	175.1
180	185.4
190	195.7
200	206.0
210	216.3
220	226.6
230	236.9
240	247.2
250	257.5
260	267.8
270	278.1
280	288.4
290	298.7
300	309.0

seawater. By examining the tables, it is seen that a diver in 170 feet of seawater experiences the same pressure as a diver in 175 feet of fresh water. A diver making a 50 foot decompression stop would have to stop at 51.5 feet in fresh water to maintain the equivalent pressure of 50 feet of seawater.

Example 3-3:

Calculate the depth of fresh water required to reach an absolute pressure of 2 atmospheres. Find the equation that expresses absolute pressure in atmospheres for depth of fresh water in feet.

Answer:

$$P_f = (.433)D_f + 14.7$$
$$2 \text{ atmospheres} = 29.4 \text{ psi}$$
$$29.4 = (.433)D_f + 14.7$$
$$D_f = \frac{14.7}{.433}$$
$$D_f = 34 \text{ feet}$$

to find absolute pressure in atmospheres
$$P = \frac{D + 34}{34}$$

[3.6]
Fresh water

where
P = absolute pressure in atmospheres
D = depth of fresh water in feet

DECOMPRESSION TABLES

When compressed air is breathed at a depth underwater, the blood and tissues of the body are exposed to elevated partial pressures of oxygen and nitrogen. Since oxygen is metabolized by the body, nitrogen is left to dissolve in the blood and tissues according to Henry's law. In order to desaturate the tissues and blood of excess nitrogen safely, it is necessary to decompress the diver in a manner which prevents bubble formation. The method proved successful is by staged decompression. Stops are made at certain intervals to allow time for dissolved nitrogen to diffuse from tissues and blood without leaving solution in the form of bubbles.

The decompression tables used in diving are based on water pressure and time of exposure. Water pressure is expressed in *feet of seawater*. The tables are explicit—there can be no interpolation. If the depth of the dive exceeds the table depth by any amount, the next deeper table must be used to calculate the decompression schedule. Decompression stop depths are given in feet of seawater. The stop depth is measured to the diver's chest. Stop depths must be accurate to assure that water pressure at the stop is sufficient. This is necessary in order to prevent nitrogen dissolved in the blood and tissues from coming out of solutions as bubbles before the blood can circulate through the lungs. In the lungs, a lower partial pressure of nitrogen in the breathing air will allow nitrogen in the blood to come out of solution safely and be exhaled.

The question arises as to the implications of different water pressures exerted in fresh water applied to the standard decompression tables. The answer is: no difference, *providing a pressure gauge calibrated in feet of seawater is used for depth measurement.* The capillary tube depth gauge and the pneumofathometer are calibrated to read out pressure in feet of seawater no matter what liquid the diver is in. A diver in 206 feet of fresh water wearing a standard depth gauge of this type will read 200 feet on his gauge and could correctly use a 200 feet decompression table even though his actual depth is 206 feet. In practice, however, many will use the 210 feet table anyway, just to be sure. If a sounding line were used to measure the bottom depth in this case, it is clear that the error would work in the diver's favor since a 210 feet table would be used. However, the decompression stop depths should not be measured by a sounding line in fresh water.

Stop depths must be at equivalent depths of seawater otherwise the diver will not be deep enough at his stop to maintain the correct water pressure on his body for the stop. This could cause the release of nitrogen bubbles in the blood and tissues resulting in decompression sickness (the bends). Because of the small differences involved, the decompression stop problem seldom arises when the stops begin above 50 feet. (See Table 3-2)

Example 3-4:

In a fresh water quarry, you lower a sounding line accurately marked every foot. The bottom of the quarry measures 245 feet exactly. When you dive to the bottom of the quarry, what will your capillary tube depth gauge read? If you make decompression stops at 50, 40, 30, 20 and 10 feet according to your capillary tube depth gauge, what depths will you observe on your sounding line?

Answer:

To find the equivalent depth of seawater:

$$P_s = P_f$$
$$(.445) D_s + 14.7 = (.433) D_f + 14.7$$
$$D_s = \frac{(.433)}{.445} D_f$$
$$D_s = (.973) D_f \qquad\qquad [3.7]$$
$$D_s = (.973) (245)$$
$$D_s = 238.4 \text{ feet}$$

The capillary tube gauge will read 238.4 feet

From Table 3-2:

Stop depth on gauge	depth on line
50 ft	51.5 ft
40 ft	41.2 ft
30 ft	30.9 ft
20 ft	20.6 ft
10 ft	10.3 ft

OTHER TYPES OF DIVING MEDIUMS

In order to evaluate diving calculations for liquids other than seawater or fresh water, it is necessary to develop general equations. A general equation can be used for any liquid once the density of the liquid is measured. A known volume of the liquid can be weighed to find the density value, then pressures and buoyancy can be predicted.

A generalized buoyancy equation is derived from Archimedes' principle. *The weight of an object wholly or partially immersed in a liquid is diminished by the weight of the liquid displaced.*

$$W_{submerged} = W_{air} - \rho_\ell V_{object}$$

where
$W_{submerged}$ = weight of object in liquid
W_{air} = weight of object in air
ρ_ℓ = density of liquid
V_{object} = volume of object submerged

When the object is completely submerged

$$W_{submerged} = V_{object} (\rho_{object} - \rho_\ell) \qquad \text{[3.8]}$$

where
$W_{submerged}$ = weight of object when submerged
V_{object} = volume of object
ρ_{object} = density of object
ρ_ℓ = density of liquid

The lifting capacity of air in any liquid (disregarding container weight and drag forces) can be found by:

$$\text{L.C.} = \rho_\ell V_{air} \qquad \text{[3.9]}$$

where

L.C. = lifting capacity of air

ρ_ℓ = density of liquid

V_{air} = volume of air

The absolute pressure in psi at any depth of any liquid at atmospheric pressure is found by

$$P_\ell = \left(\frac{\rho_\ell}{A}\right) D_\ell + 14.7$$

[3.10]

where

P_ℓ = pressure in psi exerted by liquid at depth

ρ_ℓ = density of liquid in lb/ft^3

A = 144 $\frac{in^2}{ft^2}$

D_ℓ = actual depth of liquid in ft

To find the equivalent depth of seawater:

$$P_{sea} = P_\ell$$

$$(.445)D_{sea} + 14.7 = \left(\frac{\rho_\ell}{A}\right) D_\ell + 14.7$$

$$D_{sea} = 2.25\left(\frac{\rho_\ell D_\ell}{A}\right)$$

[3.11]

where

D_{sea} = feet of seawater

ρ_ℓ = density of liquid in lb/ft^3

D_ℓ = actual depth of liquid in ft.

A = 144 $\frac{in^2}{ft^2}$

Example 3-5:
A storage tank has a broken valve. The only way to fix it is from inside the tank which is full of noncorrosive chemicals. The tank is 70 feet deep. One gallon of the liquid weighs 9-3/4 pounds. If you require a 30 pound weight belt in seawater to be neutral, what will you need in the storage tank? If you dive to the bottom of the tank, what table would you use to decompress? At what depths would your 20 feet and 10 feet stops be made? What would be your ascent rate?

Answer:

First find the density of the new liquid:

$$\rho_\ell = (9.75 \, \frac{lb}{gal}) \, (7.48 \, \frac{gal}{ft^3})$$

$$= 72.93 \, \frac{lb}{ft^3}$$

The density of seawater is:

$$\rho_s = 64.043 \, lb/ft^3$$

The excess volume the diver displaces with his dress makes his buoyancy 30 pounds positive in seawater. This excess volume will be the same in the new liquid but the weight of that excess volume of new liquid will change. The weight of the excess volume of new liquid will determine the diver's new buoyancy.

$$\rho_{sea} \, V_{excess} = 30 \, lbs$$

$$V_{excess} = \frac{30 \, lbs}{64 \, lbs/ft^3}$$

$$V_{excess} = .47 \, ft^3$$

$$\rho_\ell \, V_{excess} = \text{new weight belt}$$

$$(72.93) \, (.47) = 34.2 \, lbs$$

Easier method:

We can simply take the density ratio of the two fluids and multiple by 30 lbs

$$\text{Net weight} = (\frac{\rho_\ell}{\rho_{sea}}) \; 30 \, lbs$$

$$= (\frac{72.93}{64.043}) \, 30$$

$$= 34.2 \, lbs$$

The appropriate decompression table is found by converting the depth of the fluid into feet of seawater from Equation 3.10.

$$D_{sea} = 2.25 \, \frac{\rho_\ell \, D_\ell}{A}$$

$$= 2.25 \, \frac{(72.93) \, (70)}{144}$$

$$= 79.77 \, ft$$

use 80 ft table

10 foot stop at

$$10 = 2.25 \frac{72.93 \, (D_\ell)}{144}$$

$$D_\ell = 8.8 \text{ ft}$$

20 foot stop at

$$20 = 2.25 \frac{72.93 \, (D_\ell)}{144}$$

$$D_\ell = 17.6 \text{ ft}$$

Ascend at 60 (fsw) per min

$$60 = 2.25 \frac{72.93 \, (D_\ell)}{144}$$

$$D_\ell = 52.7$$

Ascend at 52.7 fpm

SUMMARY OF RELATIONS AND EQUATIONS
Buoyancy
Submerged weight

$$W_{sub} = W_{air} - (64.043)V$$

Seawater

$$W_{sub} = W_{air} - (62.366)V$$

Fresh water

$$W_{sub} = W_{air} - \rho_\ell V$$

Any liquid

where
W_{sub} = submerged weight of object in lbs
W_{air} = weight of object in air in lbs
V = volume of object in cubic ft
ρ_ℓ = density of liquid in lb/ft^3

Lifting capacity of air (disregarding container weight and drag)

$$\text{L.C.} = (64.043)V_a$$

Seawater

$$\text{L.C.} = (62.366)V_a$$

Fresh water

$$\text{L.C.} = \rho_\ell V_a$$

Any liquid

where
L.C. = lifting capacity in pounds
V_a = volume of air
ρ_ℓ = density of liquid

Absolute pressure at any depth

$$P_s = (.445)D_s + 14.7$$

Seawater

$$P_f = (.433)D_f + 14.7$$

Fresh water

$$P_\ell = \left(\frac{\rho_\ell}{A}\right) + 14.7$$

Any liquid

where
P_s = pressure in psi
D_s = depth of seawater in feet
P_f = pressure in psi
D_f = depth of fresh water in feet
P_ℓ = pressure in psi
D_ℓ = depth of liquid in ft
ρ_ℓ = density of liquid in lb/ft³
A = $144\dfrac{in^2}{ft^2}$

To convert depth of fresh water into feet of seawater

$$D_{sea} = .973\, D_f$$

where
D_{sea} = feet of seawater
D_f = depth of fresh water in feet

To convert depth of any liquid into feet of seawater

$$D_{sea} = \frac{(\rho_\ell D_\ell)}{A}$$

where
D_{sea} = feet of seawater
ρ_ℓ = density of liquid in lb/ft³
D_ℓ = depth of liquid in feet
A = $144\dfrac{in^2}{ft^2}$

Returning from an inspection of an 18-inch diameter oil supply pipe in 200 feet of water in the Gulf of Mexico, the diver is being assisted to the chamber to undergo surface decompression on board the barge *Chicasaw*, of Santa Fe Engineering International. He is wearing a KMB-8 Band mask by Kirby-Morgan.

CHAPTER 4: DECOMPRESSION CALCULATIONS

Accuracy is required when computing decompression schedules. It is crucial that the person making such calculations is not only accurate in his work, but also understands the process taking place in the diver's body during decompression. Any condition which could alter the decompression process must be considered and accounted for. As an example, in Chapter 3 we discussed the changes diving in fresh water or a fluid of different density from seawater can make. Other changes include diving in lakes situated at high altitudes or flying after diving, both of which seriously alter partial pressures and pressure ratios. Breathing gas mixtures used to overcome problems of oxygen toxicity and nitrogen narcosis change the amount and type of inert gas capable of dissolving in the blood and tissues. By breathing pure oxygen at decompression stops, elimination of inert gas is accelerated and decompression times can be shortened. At any depth, a dive of sufficient duration will completely saturate the body with inert gas, after which time the required decompression will remain constant. Finally, any diver encountering trouble requiring recompression must then be decompressed again at a much slower treatment rate.

To be equipped to evaluate decompression calculations, it is necessary first to examine the process of saturation and desaturation. According to Henry's law, the amount of gas that will dissolve in a liquid is almost directly proportional to the partial pressure of the gas. In the atmosphere, normal air at sea level exerts a pressure of 14.7 pounds per square inch of which approximately 80% is nitrogen and 20% is oxygen. It follows, therefore, that the amount of nitrogen dissolved in the blood and tissues at atmospheric pressure is almost directly proportional to the partial pressure of nitrogen in the atmosphere, or 11.8 psi at sea level. The amount of nitrogen dissolved in the blood and tissues at normal atmospheric pressure is, then, always constant and the body is normally saturated with nitrogen under atmospheric conditions at sea level. Oxygen, of course, is fuel for the body and is, therefore, consumed to the extent that it is not of concern during the saturation or desaturation process.

Once the normal 14.7 psi of pressure is altered, an imbalance is created between the amount of nitrogen dissolved in the body and the amount which can be dissolved due to the change of partial pressure. Because of the imbalance, it is possible for nitrogen to diffuse across alveoli membrane surfaces in the lungs. In order for balance to be restored, the blood in the body must circulate through the lung alveoli sacs enough times to absorb or discharge nitrogen in sufficient quantity to saturate or desaturate the body tissues and blood to the level of the new partial pressure. Needless to say, the complete process requires considerable time. A complicating factor is that different kinds of body tissue take up nitrogen at different rates according to the solubility of nitrogen in a particular tissue. Therefore, certain "fast" tissues may be completely saturated or desaturated in a relatively short time, perhaps minutes. Other "slow" tissues take hours to completely balance with the new partial pressure. In general, a period of 12 hours is considered sufficient time to balance the tissues with a change in higher partial pressure. Thus the body is usually considered relatively saturated with nitrogen after 12 hours exposure at the same level. However, the body is not considered completely balanced to a lower partial pressure for a period of at least 24 hours which is important to remember when considering flying after diving.

The body seems to have little or no difficulty absorbing nitrogen when exposed to higher partial pressures from diving. Tissues and blood readily dissolve nitrogen in harmless solution as long as the potential for nitrogen to dissolve exists or a balance (complete saturation) is reached. Usual dive durations do not approach the 12-hour saturation time and therefore only partially saturate some of the slower body tissues with nitrogen. The deeper the dive, the higher the concentration of nitrogen dissolved. The longer the dive, the more completely saturated the different body tissues become. A particular body tissue will become saturated at any depth within the same time period. However, the amount of nitrogen absorbed by any tissue will be higher for a deeper dive, creating a potential for oversaturation as pressure is lowered.

When ascending from exposure to higher partial pressures the process of desaturation is activated and dissolved nitrogen must be eliminated by the body the same way it came in; through the blood and tissues. Unlike saturation, desaturation can present a difficulty which the blood and tissues of the body are not equipped to handle without damage. Unfortunately, the nitrogen so readily accepted by the body is not quite so easily eliminated. Decompression imposed too rapidly upon the tissues of the body can raise the nitrogen tension so high that blood cannot carry away sufficient amounts fast enough for elimination through the lungs. Tissues and blood therefore become overloaded with a concentration of nitrogen too high for the ambient pressure to hold in solution. When the supersaturation overload reaches unstable conditions, gas bubbles begin forming in the blood and tissues of the body. Bubbles block circulation and deform tissues resulting in decompression sickness. Fortunately, a method to avoid dangerous nitrogen tension has been developed.

AIR DECOMPRESSION TABLES

The basis upon which decompression tables are established is control of the pressure *gradient* from the body tissues to the blood and lungs due to ascent. The tables take into consideration the amount of nitrogen absorbed by the body at various depths for given time periods. An allowable pressure gradient which accounts for the different gas elimination rates of different body tissues and the prevention of bubble formation is used to determine stage decompression stop depths and times. From the discussion on gas laws in Chapter 2, it has been determined that as the diver ascends from depth, the gas expansion ratios increase at shallower depths. Owing to this effect, longer and longer decompression stops are required at more frequent intervals as the surface is approached. This is done to hold the allowable pressure gradient within safe limits.

The standard air decompression tables assume the amount of nitrogen uptake by the body is due to breathing air compressed from the standard atmosphere (being approximately 80% nitrogen) at elevated partial pressures. They assume also that the diver begins descent at sea level and that his system is completely saturated with nitrogen at a partial pressure of 11.8 psi. Furthermore, it is assumed that the elevated partial pressure of the nitrogen the diver will breathe is due to the water depth in feet of *seawater*. When all these conditions are present, the Standard Air Decompression tables can be used with a reasonable degree of safety. Tables compiled by the United States Navy represent the best information available as they are the result of years of study and verification.

Breathing pure oxygen during decompression has been successfully used to shorten decompression times. Since the partial pressure of inert gas in the breathing mixture is minimized by breathing pure oxygen, the blood circulating through the lungs can dump a maximum of nitrogen in exchange for oxygen. Upon returning to the tissues, the blood is then ready to relieve them of a greater nitrogen burden than before because of the higher exchange potential. The limitation of decompression on oxygen is imposed by the toxic effect of oxygen when breathed at elevated partial pressures. The tables used by the Navy for surface decompression on oxygen take oxygen toxicity into account and demonstrate how much decompression time can safely be shortened by using pure oxygen during decompression. Some commercial diving operations have oxygen decompression tables used in the water for surface-supplied divers. In-water oxygen decompression procedures run the risk of inability to detect and treat the diver in distress from oxygen poisoning.

When decompression sickness occurs, prompt recompression is applied to control the effects of bubbles formed in tissues and blood. Unfortunately, once nitrogen has come out of solution as gas bubbles in the system, it does not return to solution very easily or quickly. Symptoms of decompression sickness can usually be alleviated by prompt recompression. The diver must then be decompressed according to a treatment table which utilizes extremely slow ascent, longer stops and oxygen when available. This allows the system to reabsorb and safely eliminate the troublesome overburden of nitrogen. The treatment tables can run considerable lengths of time depending upon the severity of the case. In some instances, symptoms will recur despite careful treatment. Subsequent follow up treatments are then necessary.

MIXED GAS DECOMPRESSION

As previously discussed, nitrogen dissolved in the blood and tissues of the body at high partial pressures presents problems of narcosis and decompression sickness. Oxygen breathed at partial pressures higher than 2 atmospheres becomes toxic to the diver's system. The problems of inert gas narcosis and absorption as well as the problem of oxygen toxicity are somewhat manageable by mixing the diver's breathing gases in proportions which alter partial pressures of the gases causing trouble.

Normal air proportions of 80% nitrogen and 20% oxygen do not present problems of oxygen toxicity at normal diving times until depths approach 297 feet. Theoretically then, at shallow working depths, the oxygen percentage of the breathing mixture can be elevated as long as the proportion of oxygen in the mix does not cause the partial pressure of oxygen at the working depth to exceed safe exposures (Tables 4-1 and 4-2). The advantage of mixing nitrogen and oxygen at higher proportions of oxygen is in lowering the nitrogen partial pressure in the breathing medium to an equivalent more shallow depth. Decompression schedules can then be calculated at the more shallow depth. In other words, the diver could theoretically breath air mixed at 60% oxygen, 40% nitrogen and decompress according to a schedule computed at half the actual dive depth because the tissues would be exposed to nitrogen partial pressures equivalent to half the actual depth. In practice, however, nitrogen-oxygen decompression is somewhat more complicated.

The partial pressure of oxygen is not to exceed 2 atmospheres under any circumstances. However, lower levels of oxygen partial pressure are not to exceed exposure limits in Tables 4-1 and 4-2. Therefore, bottom times for nitrogen-oxygen mixed gas dives must be in accordance with the limits set for exposure to oxygen partial pressure given in the table. The actual depths used in nitrogen-oxygen tables are somewhat less than theoretical depths in order to provide a margin of safety in decompression. The volume flow rate of breathing gas used is set according to conditions of exertion expected during the dive. These flow rates further alter the actual depth of the dive used in conjunction with equivalent depth.

In practice, the actual diving depth is determined, and the table corresponding to the nitrogen-oxygen mixture to be used is selected. Conditions of exertion are accounted for and appropriate volume flow rates are set. The next greater value of actual depth is used to select the equivalent air depth. Decompression is then computed according to the actual bottom time at an equivalent depth using the standard *Air Decompression Tables*. The working diver is urged to obtain these tables which are in the *U.S. Navy Diving Manual*, volume 2. See **Useful References** at the end of this book for listing. Actual bottom time in nitrogen-oxygen mixed gas dives is limited by Tables 4-1 and 4-2. The exposure time allowed by these tables will often limit the bottom time before the limits of decompression are imposed by the standard *Air Tables*. Therefore, it is not enough simply to convert to an equivalent air depth and compute decompression. Oxygen toxicity limits the bottom time of equivalent air depths and must be accounted for when computing decompression of nitrogen-oxygen mixed gas dives.

Table 4-1 Oxygen Partial Pressure Limits

(from Table 1-16, U.S. Navy Diving Manual 1970)

Exposure time (min)	Maximum Oxygen Partial Pressure (atm)
30	1.6
40	1.5
50	1.4
60	1.3
80	1.2
120	1.1
240	1.0

Table 4-2 Oxygen Partial Pressure Limits for Exceptional Exposures

(from Table 1-16a U.S. Navy Diving Manual 1970)

Exposure time (min)	Maximum Oxygen Partial Pressure (atm)
30	2.0
40	1.9
60	1.8
80	1.7
100	1.6
120	1.5
180	1.4
240	1.3

Helium-oxygen mixtures are used mainly to overcome the narcotic effect of nitrogen in deeper dives. Helium does not cause diver impairment until much greater depths. Oxygen partial pressures are regulated to avoid oxygen toxicity according to specific formulas. Helium-oxygen tables are extremely complicated due to the variety of mixtures used. Tri-mix breathing gas consisting of nitrogen, helium and oxygen is used at even greater depths. Unfortunately, some of the information regarding the use of these gas mixtures is a closely guarded industrial secret due to the expense involved in obtaining the information. A good deal of the information however is available from the U.S. Navy.

In order to properly evaluate and discuss gas mixtures and decompression to the point of utility, it would be necessary to devote an entire book to the subject. For the present time, mixed gas theory and application are best left to experts and experienced operators.

HIGH ALTITUDE DIVING AND FLYING AFTER DIVING

Recently much controversy has arisen about computing decompression schedules for diving in high altitude lakes and flying after diving. Many tables have been developed according to theory and certain assumptions. The controversy will go on until verification by testing has proven the safe use of a set of tables.

The problems presented by diving in high altitude lakes are numerous and complex. Prior to 1967 no one thought diving at high altitudes warranted any adjustment of decompression calculations. It was thought that, since the lower atmospheric pressure at high altitude caused a lower absolute pressure at depth, the use of actual measured depth would compensate for the lower atmospheric pressure at the surface; and that, since the diver would use a table for the *measured* depth and that, his equivalent depth pressure in feet of seawater would actually be less, he would not encounter decompression problems. This assumption turned out to be in error for many reasons.

The standard air decompression tables were originally developed in accordance with Haldane's theory (1922) that bends would not occur as long as the pressure reduction due to decompression was not more than one half the total pressure of the dive. After years of research and experimental verification by the U.S. Navy, it was determined that the body tissues and fluids could tolerate certain critical supersaturation *ratios* of nitrogen, the critical ratio being different for different types of body tissue. In fact, by experimental dives, the Navy developed surfacing ratios for six different tissue half-times which are the basis for the present tables. The problem which arises upon ascent from a depth at high altitude using the standard decompression tables is that critical supersaturation ratios can be exceeded due to the lower *final* atmospheric pressure. The standard air decompression tables assume that ascent is terminated at a final ambient pressure of 14.7 psi. The critical ratio is therefore based on a final pressure of 14.7 psi. A lower final pressure alters the critical *ratio*.

The use of deeper tables does not offset the critical ratio imbalance problem. Furthermore, decompression stops and ascent rates must be reevaluated.

The fact that a dive begins at a lower atmospheric pressure alters the entire pressure gradient from surface to depth of dive. Therefore, rates of ascent as well as decompression stop depths must be adjusted to account for the change in pressure gradient from standard atmospheric conditions.

Another complication arises if the diver has not been at the altitude where he begins his dive long enough for his body tissues and fluid to balance with the lower ambient pressure. If such is the case, the diver begins his descent with some degree of nitrogen tension in his tissues already, further complicating the critical ratio problem.

In addition, high altitude lakes are generally fresh water (which must also be considered, as is indicated in Chapter 3) and there exists an extremely complex set of conditions which are simultaneously affecting the already complicated problem of decompression. Needless to say, the only way to obtain reliable tables is by verified results. It is hoped these will soon be available, but in the meantime the reader is encouraged to write for information on validated tables to Human Underwater Biology, Incorporated, listed in **Useful References** at the end of this book where, also, materials on the subject of altitude diving may be consulted.

OTHER DECOMPRESSION CONSIDERATIONS

Since the U.S. Navy Decompression tables were originally tested and verified on a select group of men, it stands to reason that these tables do not account for individual differences, if any, due to sex, metabolism, diet, physical condition and other factors which are the focus of current research. Admittedly, there is a 5% error in the tables, but the error may be greater for individuals who differ markedly from the athletic male specimen, eating Navy food, by whom the tables were originally verified.

Currently, the gas exchange process between blood and tissues during saturation and desaturation is not completely understood by scientists. Therefore, many questions have been raised regarding the effect of physiological differences on decompression between men and women, as well as other individual differences.

As the results of current research are made available, it will be wise to investigate the testing and validation procedures used, if any, before implementing new methods in decompression procedure. The validation process is more important than theory when it comes to applying new ideas to the safety of divers. Indeed, the reasons why the U.S. Navy tables are so valuable is because of their long history of reliable testing and validation.

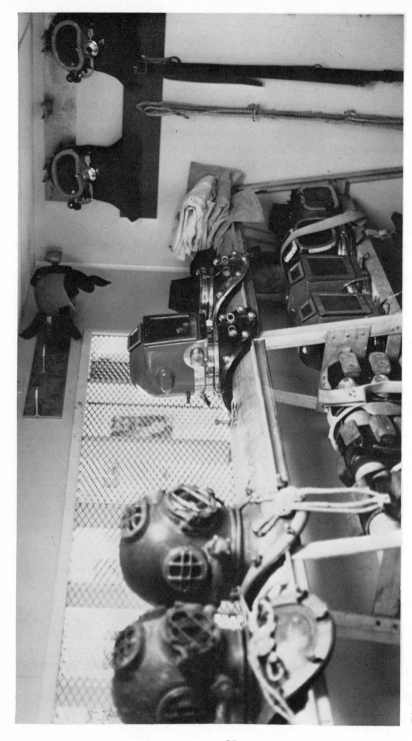

Diving locker at the Divers Training Academy, Fort Pierce, Florida. Equipment shown, l. to r. on the top shelf, MK V helmets, a Divex helmet, breast plate and neck ring, and chafing pants; on the bottom shelf, weight belts, Divex helmets, a Carson Air hat and an Aquadyne AR-1 hat; and on the wall, two KMB-9's and jocks for helmets.

CHAPTER 5: AIR SUPPLY CALCULATIONS

DIVER'S AIR SUPPLY: SCUBA

How long can a diver remain underwater with scuba equipment? Not a simple question. Several factors must be considered: the size of the scuba tank, the number of tanks carried, the actual pressure in the tank or tanks (actual tank pressure is affected by the method of filling and sometimes the dive water temperature), the depth of the dive, and the diver's breathing rate. Breathing rate depends upon the physical and mental condition of the diver, how hard he is swimming or working, and how cold he gets.

Duration of air supply is an important calculation. Miscalculation, especially on a decompression dive, could be disastrous. Planning any dive carefully requires that a diver be able to compute his air supply with all of the known conditions as accurately as possible before the dive. Then, during the dive, he must be able to adjust mentally these calculations for any unexpected change in conditions (heavier breathing rate, changes in depth, etc.). Adjustments are made by monitoring tank pressure, depth and time during the dive. The diver can make calm decisions if he knows just what that margin is and when he needs to fall back on it.

Tank size is determined by the number of surface cubic feet (scf) of air a tank holds at full pressure. The pressure required to fill a scuba tank varies for different tanks. Table 5-1 gives values for common scuba tanks.

Table 5-1
Values for Common Scuba Tanks

Tank Description	Internal Volume cubic inches	Stamped Pressure psi	Rated Pressure psi	Volume of Air Available at Rated Pressure scf
Steel 72	730	2250	2475	71.1
Aluminum 80	673	3000	3000	79.5
Aluminum 50	424	3000	3000	50.0

After the tank has cooled to air temperature from filling, and before the dive, the pressure in a scuba tank should be measured. Due to friction during the filling process, a scuba tank often becomes quite hot. The filling process should, therefore, be done slowly with the tank immersed in cool water. Through proper procedure, the amount of pressure drop upon cooling from friction heat created during filling is minimized. After cooling, the scuba tank will contain some unknown volume of air depending upon the pressure in the tank. The diver may wish to use a tank which has been partially emptied from previous use. In any case, a tank may contain less than its rated surface volume of air. To find the actual volume of surface cubic feet of air in a scuba tank at any pressure use the gas law relation:

$$V = \frac{nV_R P_G}{P_R}$$ [5.1]

where
V = actual volume of air available in tank at the surface in cubic feet
n = number of tanks
V_R = rated capacity of tank in cubic feet
P_G = gauge pressure of tank in psi
P_R = rated tank pressure in psi

Notice that for this particular problem we use gauge pressure instead of absolute pressure. This is because the residual volume of air in the tank at zero gauge pressure is unavailable to the diver.

For a steel 72 tank we find the volume of air available at the surface from Equation 5.1 and Table 5-1:

$$V_{72} = \frac{n(71.1)P_G}{2475}$$
$$V_{72} = n(.0288)P_G$$ [5.2]

where
V_{72} = volume of air available at the surface in a steel 72 tank in ft.^{3}
n = number of tanks
P_G = gauge pressure in psi

For an aluminum 80 tank

$$V_{80} = \frac{n(79.5)P_G}{(3000)}$$
$$V_{80} = n(.0265)P_G$$ [5.3]

where
V_{80} = volume of air available at the surface in an aluminum 80 tank in ft^3
n = number of tanks
P_G = gauge pressure in psi

For an aluminum 50 tank

$$V_{50} = \frac{n(50)P_G}{(3000)}$$
$$V_{50} = n(.0167)P_G$$ [5.4]

where

V_{50} = volume of air available at the surface in an aluminum 50 tank in ft^3

n = number of tanks

P_G = gauge pressure in psi

The depth of a dive will diminish the duration of the diver's air supply in scuba tanks by a factor equal to the inverse of the absolute pressure in atmospheres at that depth according to Boyle's law. Figure 5-1 displays the diminishing effect depth has on the volume of air available in a scuba tank. The relationship is found by:

$$V_D = \frac{V_s(33)}{(D+33)}$$ **[5.5]**

where

V_D = volume of air available at depth in cubic feet

V_s = surface volume of air in cubic feet from 5.1

D = depth in feet

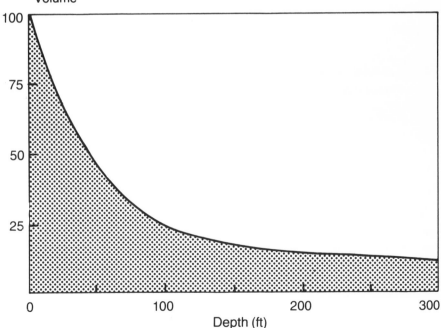

Fig. 5-1. Reduction of air supply with depth.

Temperature effects from dive water on the diver's air supply are generally ignored because they are so small. The difference between air temperature and water temperature usually does not exceed 20°F. Temperature differences of this magnitude amount to reducing air supply by less than 3%. It is conceivable, however, under rare conditions, to have a temperature difference of 55°F or more. This extreme temperature difference would reduce tank pressure by at least 10% or more. A diver with two 80 cubic foot tanks would lose 16 surface cubic feet of air under these circumstances. At a 10 foot decompression stop, the loss would reduce the available air supply by 12 minutes. Temperature effects should, therefore, not be ignored where extreme temperature differences are incurred. The temperature effect for this rare condition is found by:

$$V_T = \frac{V_D T_2}{T_1}$$

[5.6]

where

V_T = volume of air adjusted for temperature available to the diver in cubic feet

V_D = available air in cubic feet from Equation 5.5

T_2 = absolute temperature of water

T_1 = absolute temperature of air

The breathing rate of the diver is the factor most likely to be affected *during* the dive. As the diver becomes fatigued or cold, his breathing rate will increase. If he is in poor physical condition or easily excited, his breathing rate will increase drastically. For this reason, breathing rates are best estimated on individual experience. Table 5-2 gives ranges of estimated breathing rates for different circumstances. The diver should monitor his watch and tank pressure to assure air is being consumed at the estimated rate during the dive. Adjustment can be made by observing the rate of pressure drop on the gauge and mentally estimating consumption.

Generally, the rate of air consumption by a scuba diver varies between 3/4 cfm under the calmest conditions to over 4 cfm under extreme conditions of stress. For calculations under normal conditions, a diver in good physical condition will use about 1 cfm of air. Under exertion, this will rise to about 3 cfm.

The duration of air supply in minutes for scuba diving is found by dividing the volume of air available to the diver (adjusted for depth and, if necessary, for temperature) by the estimated breathing rate. For safety reasons, a minimum reserve pressure is generally observed in scuba tanks. The pressure held in reserve is usually between 300 psi and 500 psi. To find the duration of air supply in minutes in a scuba tank leaving a reserve pressure:

$$S = \frac{n V_R (P_G - P_m)(33) T_2}{R(D+33) P_R T_1}$$

[5.7]

where

S = duration of air supply in min	T_2 = absolute temperature of water
n = number of tanks	R = breathing rate in cfm
V_R = rated volume of tank in cu ft	D = depth of water in feet
P_G = gauge pressure of tank in psi	P_R = rated pressure of tank in psi
P_m = minimum reserve pressure in psi	T_1 = absolute temperature of air

Since ordinarily we disregard temperature effects, we can reduce our equation to specific tanks under normal temperature encounters.

For steel 72 tank, disregarding temperature:

$$S_{72} = \frac{n(.95)(P_G - P_m)}{R(D+33)}$$

[5.8]

where

S_{72} = duration of steel 72 tank in minutes

n   = number of tanks

P_G = gauge pressure of tank in psi

P_m = minimum reserve pressure in psi

R   = breathing rate from Table 5-2 in cfm

For aluminum 80 tank, disregarding temperature effects:

$$S_{80} = \frac{n(.875)(P_G - P_m)}{R(D+33)}$$

[5.9]

where

S_{80} = duration of aluminum 80 tank in minutes	P_m = minimum reserve pressure in psi
n = number of tanks	R = breathing rate from Table 5.2 in cfm
P_G = guage pressure of tank in psi	D = depth of dive in feet

For aluminum 50 tank, disregarding temperature effects:

$$S_{50} = \frac{n(.55)(P_G - P_m)}{R(D+33)}$$

[5.10]

where

S_{50} = duration of aluminum 50 tank in minutes

n = number of tanks

P_G = gauge pressure of tank in psi

P_m = minimum reserve pressure in psi

R = breathing rate from Table 5-2 in cfm

D = depth of dive in feet

Table 5-2 Approximate Range of Breathing Rates (scfm)

	Resting	Swimming	Working	Extreme Stress
Water 100°F	.5−.75	1.0−2.0	2.0−3.5	2.0−4+
Water 60°F	.75−1.0	1.0—2.5	2.5−3.5	3.5−4+
Water 40°F	1.0−2.0	1.0−3.0	3.0−4.0	3.5−4+

Example 5-1:

At a depth of 90 feet, a pipe flange must be bolted down. The water temperature is 50°F. The air temperature is 65°F. Your pressure gauge reads 2900 psi on your twin 80 aluminum tanks. What will be the duration of your air supply if you leave a 500 psi reserve? How many minutes would your reserve last working if you needed it? What is your maximum bottom time without using your reserve?

Answer:

$$S_{80} = \frac{n(.875)(P_G - P_m)}{R(D+33)}$$

Using a value of R = 3 from Table 5-2:

$$= \frac{2(.875)(2900-500)}{3(90+33)}$$

= 11 minutes duration with 500 psi reserve

reserve will last

$$S_{80} = \frac{n(.875)\,(500)}{3(90+33)}$$

= 2.5 min working at 90 ft

Maximum bottom time with 500 psi reserve = (duration of air supply) − (Total ascent time)

including decompression, if necessary

At 90 ft NDL. = 30 min

Total ascent for NDL. = 1:30

Max BT = 11:00 − 1:30

9:30

Example 5-2:

You have to inspect the bottom of a dam in the springtime. The lake behind the dam is fed by melting snow from the surrounding mountains. Water temperature is recorded at 40°F. Air temperature is 92°F. The bottom of the dam is measured to be 52 feet deep by pneumofathometer. You have had your twin 80 aluminum tanks charged slowly and the pressure gauge reads 3300 psi. If you leave a 300 psi reserve, will you be able to make 60 minutes bottom time? Assume diver to be warm and calm.

Answer:

Temperature must be accounted for in this example since the difference between the air and water is 52°F. Assume a calm breathing rate for inspection of 1 cfm;

$$S_{80} = \frac{n(.875)(P_G - P_m)T_2}{R(D+33)T_1}$$

$$S_{80} = \frac{2(.875)(3300-300)\,500}{1(52+33)\,552}$$

$\qquad$ = 57 min duration of air supply with 300 psi reserve

Max BT = 56 min

DIVER'S AIR SUPPLY—SURFACE SUPPLIED

Air for umbilical diving is supplied by compressor, by air flasks, or by a combination of both. Calculations to determine the size of the compressor needed or the number of air flasks required are based on three criteria: (1) the volume of air needed for breathing requirements; (2) the volume flow rate necessary to ventilate free-flow masks and helmets to avoid CO_2 buildup; and (3) the air pressure required to overcome water pressure at the depth of the dive as well as pressure losses through hoses and fittings with adequate reserve pressure (over bottom pressure) to prevent squeeze from falling.

Surface supplied diving apparatus is either free-flow type where the breathing gas is continuously flowing through the mask or helmet, or it is demand type where the breathing gas is supplied directly on breathing demand, then immediately exhausted into the water. The air requirements are calculated differently for each type of apparatus since the flow rates, and consequently, the system pressures must meet different criteria. On the one hand, air for the free-flow apparatus must meet a continuous volume flow rate to avoid CO_2 buildup in the helmet or mask.

On the other hand, demand type apparatus, must be able to meet the instantaneous peak flow rate requirement for the inhalation cycle of the diver's breathing. This maximum flow rate is not a continuous demand (over the cycle of breathing, the overall volume requirement of air averages out to be the same as for free-flow) but the system must be able to provide the maximum instantaneous flow when, and for as long as it is required. The system must, therefore, be able to replace the air consumed from that system at a rate sufficient to maintain the required pressure.

When the diver breathes air from a demand supply, each breath activates a demand regulator which provides the diver with fresh respirable gas. When the diver exhales, the used air containing CO_2, is exhausted through a one-way valve into the water. Then, the next breath drawn is new, fresh breathing gas. However, when the diver is breathing air inside a helmet or free-flow mask, his exhaled gas does not go directly out into the water, but mixes with the gas inside his helmet or mask. This mixture introduces a level of carbon dioxide into the diver's breathing medium. Therefore, the air space in the helmet, or mask, must be flushed continously to prevent CO_2 from reaching toxic levels.

During the normal metabolic process, oxygen is taken up by the blood in the lungs and carried by arteries to the tissues of the body where it is metabolized. A by-product of the metabolization process is CO_2 which is removed from the tissues by veinal blood, carried to the lung capillaries, and exhausted into the air. The elimination of CO_2 from the body in this manner is contingent upon the lower partial pressure of CO_2 in the surrounding atmosphere. If the surrounding partial pressure of CO_2 is too high, the lungs will not be able to wash out excess CO_2 which then accumulates in the body resulting in acidosis. Since the breathing cycle is triggered to an extent by the partial pressure of CO_2 in the blood, the breather will begin to gasp, undergo severe headaches, become dizzy and then become unconscious.

The recommended nontoxic limit of CO_2 in the diver's breathing medium is .02 atmospheres partial pressure, (about 2% at the surface). The amount of CO_2 the diver produces is proportional to his oxygen uptake or how hard he is working. It happens that the volume flow rate necessary to ventilate the diver's helmet properly will also provide an adequate volume for breathing requirements. The exact air flow required to ventilate a particular type of helmet or mask can be calculated if the gas-mixing effectiveness parameters of the apparatus are known. However, there are certain parameters involved in the calculation which must be determined by experiment and air quality sampling devices. Therefore, it serves most commercial purposes to select a value which assures adequate ventilation under extreme circumstances. The volume flow rate used to ventilate most types of apparatus under normal conditions is 4.5 actual cubic feet per minute per diver at the surface.

The smaller type of diving helmet such as the Navy MK XII requires a higher volume flow rate under conditions of exertion to assure proper flushing of CO_2. The smaller helmet volume allows more rapid CO_2 buildup under the right conditions. To assure proper ventilation, 6 acfm per diver at the surface is used for the MK XII type helmet where conditions of extreme exertion are anticipated. This rate insures with reasonable certainty that a toxic level of CO_2 will not be reached.

The volume flow rate to ventilate surface supplied diving apparatus is found by:

$$S = 4.5N \frac{D+33}{33}$$

[5.11]

For most apparatus under normal dive conditions

$$S = 6N \frac{D+33}{33}$$

[5.12]

For smaller helmets under extreme exertion

where
S = flow rate of air supply in surface cubic feet per min
N = number of divers
D = depth of dive in feet

An air system must also be able to deliver the required volume flow rate at a continuous pressure. Pressure must be high enough to overcome water pressure and pressure losses through hoses and fittings. Further, adequate reserve or overbottom pressure must be available to prevent squeeze injury in the event of a fall. In most free-flow apparatus, the required pressure can be achieved by adding 50 psi over the bottom pressure for depths up to 120 feet. After 120 feet, 100 psi over the bottom pressure is used. Therefore:

$$OVB = (.445)D + \begin{matrix} 50 \text{ where } D < 120\,\text{ft} \\ 100 \text{ where } D \geq 120\,\text{ft} \end{matrix}$$

[5.13]

where
OVB = required pressure for compressor in psi using free flow apparatus
D   = depth of dive in feet

For the U. S. Navy (Mark V) deep sea diving dress, the pressure equation is modified by the Navy to:

$$P_{MKV} = 25 + (0.71)D$$

[5.14]

where
P_{MKV} = manifold pressure in psi for MK V
D   = depth of dive in feet

Equation 5.14 yields somewhat lower pressure requirements than 5.13 and is evidently used *only* in conjunction with MK V operations.

Pressure requirements for U S Navy MK XII diving helmets are given as follows:

$$\begin{aligned} P_{MK\,XII} &= (0.5)D + 42 \text{ for 200 ft hose} \\ &= (0.62)D + 42 \text{ for 600 ft hose} \end{aligned}$$

[5.15]

where
$P_{MK\,XII}$ = manifold pressure in psi for MK VII
D   = depth of dive in feet

For pressure requirement to be adequate for demand apparatus to operate from compressors, the peak volume flow requirement must be met without suffering a pressure drop below safe levels. The average volume flow requirement will be the same as free-flow, but the instantaneous peak flow rate will exceed the average. Therefore, since compressors operate on a continuous rather than intermittent basis, the easiest way to insure that air is replaced at a rate sufficient to maintain the required pressure is to elevate the manifold pressure so that it never drops below the normal overbottom pressure. The safe manifold pressure for demand apparatus according to the U.S. Navy is:

$$P = (.445)D + 135 \qquad\qquad \textbf{[5.17]}$$

where

P = manifold pressure for demand apparatus in psi
D = depth of dive in feet

Note:

At deeper dives, pressure may have to be elevated as diver descends in order to prevent demand system from free flowing.

Compressors for diving must meet the following capacity requirements:

1. Volume flow rate in cfm for all systems must be at least that given by Equation 5.12.
    Caution: Commercial compressors specify capacity in either displacement cfm or cfm of free air. Displacement cfm does not reflect the efficiency of the compressor and is not the actual amount of air delivered by the compressor. The actual delivery of a compressor is specified in cfm of free air at a specified pressure. As the operating pressure of the compressor is increased, the efficiency declines and the cfm of free air is less.
2. The compressor must be able to deliver air at the minimum flow rate operating at or above the pressure given by Equation 5.13 for free flow apparatus or Equation 5.17 for demand apparatus.

Table 5-3 tabulates minimum air system requirements per diver. Where conditions of stress or extreme temperature are anticipated, consult equations and allow a safety factor.

Table 5-3
Minimum Air System Requirements per Diver for Normal Working Conditions

Depth (FSW)	Minimum volume flow (cfm) (See Equation 5.11)	Free-Flow minimum manifold pressure (psig) (See Equation 5.13)	Demand minimum manifold pressure (psig) (See Equation 5.17)
10	6	55	140
20	8	60	145
30	9	65	150
40	10	70	155
50	12	75	160
60	13	80	165
70	14	85	170
80	16	90	175
90	17	95	180
100	19	100	180
110	20	100	185
120	21	155	190
130	23	160	195
140	24	165	200
150	25	170	205
160	27	175	210
170	28	180	215
180	29	185	220
190	31	190	220
200	32	195	225

Note: Consult Equations 5.11 through 5.17 to determine specific air requirements.

Example 5-3:

Two divers using free flow masks will dive to 140 fsw. Will a compressor which delivers 50 cfm at 170 psi be adequate?

Answer:

Volume flow check:

$$S = \frac{4.5N(D+33)}{33}$$

$$= \frac{4.5(2)(140+33)}{33}$$

$$= 47.2 \text{ cfm}$$

Yes

pressure check for D ≥ 120:

$$OVB = (.445)D + 100$$
$$= (.445)(140) + 100$$
$$= 162.3 \, psi$$

Yes

High pressure air flasks are often used in surface supplied diving operations. One distinct advantage to a system of air flasks is the elimination of compressor noise which interferes with communications and video camera operations. Also, air flasks virtually provide a fail safe backup system for use with compressors.

When high pressure air flasks are charged, a small amount of contaminants and water vapor will always enter the flasks. These contaminants will tend to concentrate and settle. Consequently, as the end of the air supply is reached the contaminants will begin to discharge into the diver's air. For this reason, a minimum pressure in the working flasks is set at 220 psi in excess (over bottom) of the pressure at which the divers are working. This minimum pressure is observed so as not to dump the concentration of contaminants into the diver's air supply.

The duration of a system of air flasks is then determined by the following equation:

$$T = \frac{CN[A - (15 + E + 1)]}{4.5 \, n \, (E + 1)}$$

[5.19]

where

T = time in minutes
C = internal volume of one flask in cubic feet (when discharged)
N = number of flasks (minus one for reserve if a secondary air supply is not available)

A = gauge pressure of air in the flasks in atmospheres (psi divided by 14.7)
E = gauge pressure at depth to which dive is to be made in atmospheres (D/33)
n = number of divers

If decompression will be required, the length of time spent on the bottom must be reduced to allow sufficient air for decompression. The amount of air required for decompression is the sum of the cubic feet of air used at each stop per diver:

$$V = (\frac{SD}{33} + 1) \, 4.5 \, T_{SD}$$

[5.20]

where
V   = volume of air used at stop in surface cubic feet per diver
SD = stop depth in feet
T_{SD} = duration of time at stop plus ascent time from preceeding stop in min

The number of minutes by which the bottom time is reduced per diver is then found by:

$$T_R = \frac{(\Sigma V)\,D}{4.5\,(D+33)}$$ [5.21]

where
T_R = reduction of bottom time in minutes per diver
ΣV = sum of cubic feet of air used for ascent and decompression from [5.20]
D = depth of dive in feet

Example 5-4:

One diver is to descend to 210 fsw on a bank of 10 air flasks. Each flask has a capacity of 300 cubic feet of free air when charged to 3,000 psi. The gauge pressure of the 10 bank system is 2800 psi. A dive is planned for a bottom time of 15 minutes. No backup system is available. Is the system adequate?

Answer:

Use air decompression tables and compute decompression requirements:

$$V = (\frac{SD}{33} + 1)\,4.5\,T_{SD}$$

$$V_{30} = (\frac{30}{33} + 1)\,4.5\,(1+3) = 34.4\ ft^3$$

$$V_{20} = (\frac{20}{33} + 1)\,(4.5)\,(5 + 1/6) = 34.7\ ft^3$$

$$V_{10} = (\frac{10}{33} + 1)\,(4.5)\,(13 + 1/6) = 77.2\ ft^3$$

$$\Sigma V = 149\ ft^3$$

Compute reduction of bottom time

$$T_R = \frac{(\Sigma V)D}{4.5(D + 33)}$$

$$= \frac{(149)(210)}{4.5(210+33)}$$

$$= 29 \text{ min}$$

Compute bottom time

$$T = \frac{CN[A - (15 + E + 1)]}{4.5n (E + 1)}$$

The internal volume C of a flask with a capacity of 300 cubic feet at 3,000 psi is found by

$$C = V_v \left(\frac{P_2}{P_1}\right) = 300 \left(\frac{15}{3015}\right) = 1.5 \text{ ft}^3$$

$$T = \frac{1.5(9) \left[\frac{2800}{14.7} - (15 + \frac{210}{33} + 1)\right]}{4.5 (1) \left(\frac{210}{33} + 1\right)}$$

$$= \frac{1.5(9)(167.6)}{(4.5)(7.4)}$$

$$= 68 \text{ min}$$

Now subtract decompression time

$$68 - 29 = 39 \text{ min}$$

Answer:
Yes, there is more than enough air for 15 min bottom time at 210 feet allowing for decompression and reserve.

SUMMARY OF RELATIONS AND EQUATIONS

Scuba
Duration of air supply in scuba tanks in general:

$$S = \frac{nV_R (P_G - P_m) (33) (T_2)}{R (D + 33) P_R T_1}$$

where

S = duration of air supply in min

n = number of tanks

V_R = rated volume of tank in cu ft

P_G = gauge pressure of tank in psi

P_m = minimum reserve pressure in psi

T_2 = absolute temperature of water in °R

R = breathing rate in cfm

D = depth of dive in feet

P_R = rated pressure of tank in psi

T_1 = absolute temperature of air °R

Duration of steel 72 disregarding temperature:

$$S_{72} = \frac{n(.95)(P_G - P_m)}{R(D+33)}$$

where

S_{72} = duration of steel 72 in min

n = number of tanks

P_G = gauge pressure of tank in psi.

P_m = minimum reserve pressure in psi

R = breathing rate in cfm

D = depth of dive in ft

Duration of aluminum 80 disregarding temperature:

$$S_{80} = \frac{n(.875)(P_G - P_m)}{R(D + 33)}$$

where

S_{80} = duration of aluminum 80 in min

n = number of tanks

P_G = gauge pressure of tank in psi

P_m = minimum reserve pressure in psi

R = breathing rate in cfm

D = depth of dive in ft

Surface Supply

Volume flow rate to ventilate surface supplied diving:

$$S = 4.5N \left(\frac{D+33}{33} \right)$$

where

S = flow rate of air supply in surface scfm

N = number of divers

D = depth of dive in ft

Pressure required for free flow apparatus:

$$OVB = (.445)D + \begin{array}{l} 50 \text{ where } D < 120 \text{ ft} \\ 100 \text{ where } D \geq 120 \text{ ft} \end{array}$$

where
OVB = required pressure for compressor in psi using free flow apparatus
D   = depth of dive in ft

Pressure for demand apparatus:

$$P = (.445)D + 135$$

where
P = manifold pressure for demand apparatus in psi
D = depth of dive in ft

Duration of air flasks:

$$T = \frac{CN[A - (15 + E + 1)]}{4.5n(E + 1)}$$

where

T = time in min

C = capacity of one flask in cu ft of free air

N = number of flasks (minus one for reserve where secondary air supply is not available)

A = gauge pressure of air in the flasks in atmosphere (psi divided by 14.7)

n = number of divers

E = gauge pressure at depth of dive in atmospheres (D/33)

Volume of air required for decompression:

$$V = (\frac{SD}{33} + 1)\, 4.5\, T_{SD}$$

where

V = volume of air used at stop in surface cubic ft per diver

S_D = stop depth in ft

T_{SD} = duration of time at stop plus ascent time from preceeding stop in min

Reduction of bottom time to allow for decompression:

$$T_R = \frac{(\Sigma V)D}{4.5(D+33)}$$

where
T = duration of bottom
ΣV = sum of cu ft of air used for ascent and decompression
D = bottom depth in ft

CHAPTER 6: BUOYANCY AND THE DIVER[†]

Archimedes' principle states: *Any object wholly or partially immersed in a liquid is buoyed up by a force equal to the weight of liquid displaced.*

Which is heavier: 10 pounds of lead or 10 pounds of concrete? If weighed in air, each weighs the same. But, if taken underwater, the lead weighs more than the concrete. Why?

Lead is denser than concrete; therefore, it occupies less volume. In turn, the lead displaces less water; so there is a smaller force of buoyancy acting on the lead. The force of buoyancy on a submerged object equals the weight of water the object displaces. This force is subtracted from the true or "air" weight of the object to give its weight underwater.

Water weighs about 64 pounds per cubic foot (salt water weighs 64.043 lbs/ft^3, fresh water weighs 62.366 lbs/ft^3). If an object having a volume of 1 cubic foot is placed in water and sinks, it weighed more than 64 pounds, in air and weighs less than 64 pounds underwater.

If a 1 cubic foot object weighing less than 64 pounds is placed in the water, it floats. Part of it remains above water and part of it below. The part below water displaces an amount of water equalling the weight of the object. For example, suppose 1 cubic foot of cork weighs 16 pounds. It floats with three quarters of its volume above water and one-quarter below (one-quarter of a cubic foot of water weighs 16 pounds).

What happens if enough weight is placed on the cork to submerge it? It displaces a cubic foot of water and then has a 48 pound lifting capacity if the weight is removed.

Suppose a cubic foot of a substance weighs exactly 64 pounds? It is neutral underwater. It neither sinks nor floats, remaining suspended at any level it is placed.

What does this mean to the diver? Scuba divers are aware of the advantage of neutral buoyancy. It is easier to maneuver underwater if one is "weightless." It is not so easy to attain and maintain neutral buoyancy, however. A scuba diver is never a constant-volume object. The amount of water he displaces is always changing. How can this be?

A scuba diver underwater is constantly changing the volume of his lungs by breathing. This alters the volume of the diver between inhalation and exhala-

---

[†]By permission of *Skin Diver* magazine.

tion. Therefore, the force of buoyancy fluctuates while the weight of the diver remains essentially constant. The diver is then alternately "heavy" and "light" but never quite neutral (as long as he is breathing).

Something else happens to the scuba diver. As he breathes the air from his tank, the weight of the tank decreases. So the total weight of the diver slowly decreases over the duration of the dive. This decrease is a small amount, but neutral buoyancy is sensitive to minute changes. Near the end of the dive, the diver may notice he tends to rise more than he did at the start.

The diver wearing a wetsuit encounters another problem. He weighs himself to overcome the buoyancy of the wetsuit, but as he descends, the suit is compressed so it occupies less volume than it did at the surface. Hence, the diver notices an increasing tendency to sink as he goes deeper. Many divers blow a little air in their life vest (or "buoyancy compensator") to overcome this. This works well if the diver remains at that depth, but if he ascends or descends a few feet, the volume of air in his vest changes and again alters his buoyancy. For this reason, the unisuit diver probably has the best system for buoyancy control. He can put on an excess of weight and continuously adjust his buoyancy by pushing buttons which increase or decrease his suit volume with air.

Overcoming the negative buoyancy of sugmerged objects with air has stirred the imagaination of many divers. However, lifting large objects underwater involves many complex considerations. Calculation must be made of the weight of the submerged object. Many sunken objects are not solid and many are made of more than one material. At any depth, the buoyant force of the initial volume of air necessary to lift an object from the bottom exceeds the weight of the object due to the reactive forces (suction) between the object and the bottom. The amount of reaction depends on the area of the object in contact with the bottom, how much of the object is buried, and the type of bottom encountered (mud, rock, sand, etc.).

Air weighs so little compared to an equal volume of water that it virtually lifts the same as it displaces, 64 pounds per cubic foot. But air must be contained in something strong enough to lift the object. The weight of the container must then be subtracted from the lifting capacity. Drag friction on the rising container against the water must be accounted for, and if the rising object presents a large surface area, drag friction of the object must also be considered.

Finally, according to Boyle's law, since air will expand upon rising, the container must either be strong enough to withstand the increase in pressure, or it must vent the excess pressure. If the container is itself expandable, the object will accelerate as it rises. This is undesirable because there is no control; and the object may hit the surface so fast that it leaves the water and is damaged when it comes down again, breaking lines, sinking or bursting the container. This phenomenon explains why the better life vests have a relief valve.

A student diver at Divers Training Academy, Fort Pierce, Florida, dressed in an advanced Swindell (Divex) helmet and unisuit. He has inflated his suit to attain positive buoyancy in order to navigate on the water's surface.

UNDERWATER WEIGHT

The weight of an object in air is found by multiplying object density and object volume.

$$W_{air} = \rho_o V_o \qquad \text{[6.1]}$$

where
W_{air} = weight of object in air in pounds
ρ_o = density of object in pounds per cubic foot
V_o = volume of object in cubic feet

In order to calculate the weight of a submerged object, the weight of the volume of water displaced by the object must be subtracted from its air weight according to Archimedes' principle;

$$W_{sub} = \rho_o V_o - {}_w V_o$$
$$W_{sub} = V_o (\rho_o - \rho_w) \qquad \text{[6.2]}$$

where
W_{sub} = weight of object under water in lbs
V_o = volume of object in cubic feet
ρ_o = density of object in lbs/ft³
ρ_w = density of water

Example 6-1:
What is the weight of a block of concrete measuring 18 in x 12 in x 9 in? How much will it weigh under seawater?
Answer:

$$W = \rho V$$
$$\rho = 150 \text{ lb/ft}^3 \text{ from Table 6-1}$$
$$V = \frac{(18)(12)(9) \text{ in}^3}{1728 \text{ in}^3/\text{ft}^3} = 1.125 \text{ ft}^3$$
$$W = (150)(1.125)$$
$$= 168.75 \text{ lbs.}$$

Under seawater

$$W_{sub} = V(\rho_o - \rho_w)$$
$$V = 1.124 \text{ ft}^3$$
$$\rho_o = 150 \text{ lbs/ft}^3$$
$$\rho_w = 64.043 \text{ lbs/ft}^3$$
$$W_{sub} = 1.125(150-64)$$
$$= 96.7 \text{ lbs}$$

Example 6-2:

Calculate the under seawater weight of the same block of concrete with 36 18 in x 1/2 in diameter steel rebars imbedded in the block. (Fig. 6-1)

Answer:

$$W_{sub} = V_{conc}(\rho_{conc} - \rho_w) + V_{steel}(\rho_{steel} - \rho_w)$$

$$V_{conc} = V_{block} - V_{steel}$$

$$V_{steel} = \frac{36(\pi(1/4)^2\ 18)}{1728} = 0.74\ ft^3$$

$$V_{block} = 1.125\ ft^3$$

$$V_{conc} = V_{block} - V_{steel}$$

$$V_{conc} = 1.051\ ft^3$$

$$W_{sub} = (1.05)(150\text{-}64) + (.074)(485\text{-}64)$$

$$= 90.3 + 31.2$$

$$= 121.5\ lbs$$

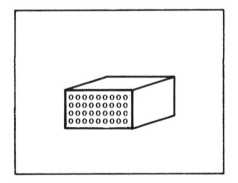

Fig. 6-1. Concrete block with 36 rebars embedded.

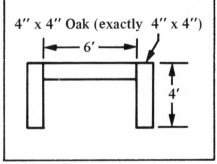

4" x 4" Oak (exactly 4" x 4")

6'

4'

Fig. 6-2. Oak frame.

Example 6-3:

The wooden frame diagrammed (Fig. 6-2) is to be used under seawater as a form to pour concrete. Calculate how many 20 lb lead weights must be attached to give it a negative buoyancy of at least 20 lbs. How many 20 lb concrete weights?

Answer:

14 linear ft of 4 in x 4 in oak

$$V = (\frac{16}{144})(14)\,ft^3$$

$$= 1.56\,ft^3$$

$$\rho_o = 44\,lbs/ft^3$$

$$W_{sub} = V(\rho_o - \rho_w)$$

$$= (1.56)(44-64)$$

$$= 31\,lbs$$

Therefore the frame has a buoyancy of 31 lbs.
Need to add 31 + 20 = 51 lbs to get negative buoyancy of 20 lbs.
The density of lead = 708 lb/ft^3

$$\text{Volume of } = \frac{20}{708} = .028\,ft^3$$
$$\text{20 lbs lead}$$

$$W_{sub} = .028\,(708-64) = 18.2\,lbs$$

use three 20# lead weights

$$\text{Density of concrete} = 150\,lb/ft^3$$

$$\text{Volume of } = \frac{20}{150} = .13\,ft^3$$
$$\text{20 lbs}$$

$$W_{sub} = .13(150-64)$$

$$= 11.2\,lbs$$

use five 20# concrete weights

LIFTING CALCULATIONS

The use of air in overcoming negative buoyancy is widely applied in underwater work. Since air weighs virtually zero compared to an equal volume of water, its lifting capacity will equal the weight of the water it displaces. Air, however, must be suitably contained in order to make it useful for lifting operations. A strong container will usually have appreciable weight which must be subtracted from the lifting capacity of the air. As an object moves through the water, the water must flow around it. Water will resist the motion of a rising container and cause a drag force. If the object being lifted presents a surface area which is large enough, it too will be subject to drag forces. In general, however:

$$L.C. = (\rho_w V_c)(C_D) - W_c \qquad \text{[6.3]}$$

where
LC = lifting capacity in lbs
ρ_w = density of water in lb/ft^3
V_c = volume of container in ft^3
C_D = coefficient of drag
W_c = weight of container in lbs

For most lifting calculations,
C_D = .75
ρ_w = 64 lb/ft^3 seawater
ρ_w = 62 lb/ft^3 fresh water

When the container rises to the surface, it will be partly out of the water. We therefore use the air weight of the container for W_c since it will be partly in air at the end of the lift.

$$\text{Seawater LC} = 48\, V_c - W_c \qquad\qquad \textbf{[6.4]}$$
$$\text{Fresh water LC} = 46.5\, V_c - W_c \qquad\qquad \textbf{[6.5]}$$

where
LC = lifting capacity in lbs
V_c = volume of container
W_c = weight of container

Example 6-4:
If a 55 gallon drum weighs 20 lb, what is its lifting capacity in seawater?
Answer:
$$V_c = (55\,\text{gal})(.1337\,\text{ft}^3/\text{gal}) = 7.35\,\text{ft}^3$$
$$W_c = 20\,\text{lbs}$$
$$LC = 48(V_c) - W_c$$
$$LC = (48)(7.35) - 20$$
$$= 333\,\text{lbs}$$

Example 6-5:
A hollow steel ball 8 ft in diameter by 1/4 in thick will be used to lift an old winch weighing 5 tons under seawater. Does it have the capacity?
Answer:
Weight of ball = (surface area)(thickness)(density of steel)

$$= (4\pi r^2)(1/4 \text{ in } \frac{1}{12} \text{ ft/in})(485 \text{ lb/ft}^3)$$

$$= (4\pi(4^2)(\frac{1}{48})(485)$$

$$= 2{,}032 \text{ lbs}$$

Volume of ball $= 4/3\pi r^3$

$$= 268 \text{ ft}^3$$

$$LC = (48)(268) - 2032$$

$$= 12{,}864 - 2032$$

$$= 10{,}832 \text{ lbs}$$

$$= 5.4 \text{ tons}$$

Yes

Example 6-6:

A sunken fishing boat is to be salvaged. The plan is to lighten the boat with air, then lift her off the bottom by winches. During the survey it was observed that the boat rested on hard bottom. The winch capacity will therefore be able to break the ground force and start the lift. Your job is to lighten the boat until she is almost neutral. Out of the water on the railway, the boat weighed 20 tons. She is essentially all steel. If you are to lighten her to 2 tons, how many 1,000 gallon steel fuel drums weighing 1 ton each will be required?

Answer:

The fuel drums will not be lifting the boat, only lightening it. Therefore, the drag forces will be taken up by the winches and the lightening force of the fuel drums will become;

$$(64)(V_c) - W_c$$

The weight of 20 tons of steel underwater is;

$$\frac{40{,}000 \text{ lbs}}{485 \text{ lbs/ft}^3} = 82.5 \text{ ft}^3$$

$$82.5 \text{ ft}^3 (485 - 64) = 34{,}733 \text{ lbs}$$

We want to reduce this weight to 2 tons, therefore the fuel drums must lighten the ship by

$$34{,}733 - 4000 = 30{,}733 \text{ lbs}$$

$$30{,}733 = (64(1000)(.1357) - 2{,}000)(\text{number of drums})$$

$$30{,}733 = (6557)n$$

$$n = 4.69$$

use 5 drums

Table 6-1 Table of Density Values

Material	Density (16/ft³)	Material	Density (16/ft³)
Gold	1205	Aluminum	169
Mercury	845	Concrete	150
Lead	708	Magnesium	108
Silver	655	Seawater	64.043
Copper	559	Fresh Water	62.366
Brass	514	Oak Wood (dry)	44
Steel	485	Pine Wood (dry)	27
Zinc	445	Balsa Wood (dry)	8
Granite	170	Styrofoam	1

Table 6-2
Weights of Various Materials

Material	Weight per Cubic Foot, Pounds	Material	Weight per Cubic Foot, Pounds
Air	0.0807	Carbon Dioxide	0.1227
Alcohol	50	Carbon Disulfide	80.6
Aluminum	168	Carbon Monoxide	0.0781
Ammonia	0.0478	Carpets and Rugs	30
Antimony	415	Cement, Portland	94
Arsenic	358	Cement, Portland (Set)	155
Asbestos	125-175	Chalk	137
Ashes and Cinders, Packed	40-45	Charcoal	20-35
		Chromium	428
Asphalt	69-94	Clay (Dry)	120-140
		Clay (Wet)	165-195
Barley, Bulk	31	Coal, Anthracite	97
Basalt, Piled	96	Coal, Bituminous	84
Bauxite	159	Cobalt	552
Benzene	56	Coke	75
Books, Packed	65	Concrete Masonry, Plain	145
Borax	109	Concrete Masonry, Reinforced	150
Brass	524		
Brick, Common	112	Copper	554
Bronze, Metal	544	Copper Ore	262
Cadmium	539	Cork	16
Canned Goods, Cases	58	Corn, Bulk	37
Carbolic Acid (15°C)	59.2-60.2	Cotton, Bales, Compressed	25
Carbon, Amorphous	130		

(Continued)

87

Table 6-2 Weights of Various Materials (Continued)

Material	Weight per Cubic Foot, Pounds	Material	Weight per Cubic Foot, Pounds
Dry Rubble Masonry, Granite	130	Jute, Bales, Compressed	41
		Kerosene	51
Earth, Excavated, Packed	105	Lead	708
Earth, Loose	80	Lead Ore, Galena	465
Emery	250	Leather	59
Ethane, C_2H_6	0.0847	Lime, Mortar	103-111
Excelsior, Bales, Compressed	19	Lime, Slaked	81-87
		Limestone	167-171
Feldspar	159-172	Linen, Dry Goods, Cases	35-50
Ferro-Silicon	437	Lye Soda 66%	106
Fir, Seasoned	30-44	Magnesite	187
Flour	47	Magnesium	109
Flourite	198	Magnetite	306-324
Gas, Natural	0.028-0.036	Malachite	231-256
Gasoline	41-43	Manganese	460
Glass	180-196	Manganese Ore, Loosely Piled	165-200
Glycerine (0°C)	78.6	Manganese Ore, Pyrolusite	259
Gravel	100-120	Marble	160-177
Gypsum, Alabaster	159	Marble, Quarried, Loosely Piled	95
Hay, Bales, Compressed	24	Meat, Barrels	37
Helium	0.0112	Mercury (15.6°C)	847
Hemp, Bales, Compressed	22	Methane, CH_4	0.0447
Hides, Raw, Bales, Compressed	23	Mica	165-200
Hydrochloric Acid, Gas, HCL	0.1023	Molasses, Barrels	48
		Molybdenum	560
Hydrochloric Acid, Liquid, HCL	74.8	Mortar Rubble, Granite, Limestone, Marble	150-155
Hydrogen, H_2	0.0056	Mortar Rubble, Bluestone, Sandstone	130
Hydrogen Sulfide, H_2S	0.0950	Muriatic Acid 40%	75
Ice	57		
Iron, Cast	450	Naphtha (15°C)	41.5
Iron Ore, Hematite	325	Nickel	545
Iron Ore, Hematite Loose	150	Nitrates, Loosely Piled	100
Iron Ore, Hematite In Bank	170	Nitric Oxide, NO	0.0836
Iron Ore, Limonite	237	Nictric Acid 91%	94
Iron Ore, Magnetite	315	Nitrogen, N_2	0.0784
Iron, Wrought	485	Nitrous Oxide, N_2O	0.1234

Table 6-2 Weights of Various Materials (Continued)

Material	Weight per Cubic Foot, Pounds	Material	Weight per Cubic Foot, Pounds
Oak, White	44	Silk, Goods In Bulk	45
Oats, Bulk	26	Silver	655
Oils, Mineral	58	Slag	70-100
Oil, Vegetable	57	Slate, Shale	162-205
Oxygen, O_2	0.0892	Soapstone, Talc	169
		Snow, Loosely Piled	35
Paper	58	Steel	485
Paraffin	54-57	Stone, Loosely Piled	75
Petroleum, Crude	55	Straw, Bales, Compressed	19
Petroleum, Refined	50	Sulphur	125
Phosphate Rock, Loosely Piled	60	Sulphur Dioxide, SO_2	0.1827
Pine, Yellow	44	Sulphuric Acid 87%	112
Pitch	72	Tallow	58
Plaster of Paris	74-80	Tar, Bituminous	75
Porcelain, China	150	Tin	458
Potatoes, Bulk	44	Tin Ore, Cassiterite	418
Pumice, Natural	40	Tungsten	1180
Quartz, Quarried, Loosely Piled	95	Turpentine (16°C)	54.2
Quartzite	170	Water, (Freezing Point) 0°C	62.417
Rags, Bales, Compressed	19	Water, (Maximum Density) 4°C	62.425
Resins, Rosin	67	Water, (Standard) (62°F) 16.7°C	62.354
Riprap, Limestone	80-85		
Riprap, Sandstone	90	Water, 20°C	62.315
River Mud	90	Water, 100°C	59.70
Rubber	58	Water, Sea (62°F) 16.78°C	63.936
Rye, Bulk	48		
		Wax	60
Salt, Ground In Sacks	60	Wood, Bales, Compressed	48
Sand	90-100		
Shale, Loosely Piled	92	Zinc	440
Silicon	155	Zinc Ore, Blended	453

Diver inspecting a 200-foot supply barge sunk in 80 feet of water off St. Croix in the Caribbean.

CHAPTER 7: SALVAGE CALCULATIONS

Damage and flooding control on a sinking vessel are immediate problems to the working salvage diver. Every effort must be made to "hold fast" in order to avoid sinking.

Calculations of pressure on submerged parts of the work, volume flow rate of water through a hole in a sinking ship, strength of patches, pumping requirements, air supply requirements for tools, and buoyancy are calculations of major concern to the salvage diver which are often made on the spot. Raising a sunken ship allows more time for initial survey and calculations, but sometimes requires crucial calculations during the salvage attempt to account for unforeseen circumstances. Salvage practice encompasses many situations which are beyond the scope of this book. However, salvage calculations which directly concern the working diver should be in the realm of his understanding in order that he may provide accurate and complete survey information and, where necessary, make his own calculations.

DAMAGE AND FLOODING

If a sinking ship can be salvaged before it goes under, great expense and effort can be avoided. Damage and flood control are often dependent upon the diver's ability to assess the damage correctly, and make appropriate repairs in time. Water pressure calculations on any part of the damaged ship underwater can be made. The force on patches, watertight bulkheads, and decks behind flooded or partially flooded compartments can be determined to evaluate patches and shoring requirements. For these calculations to be made properly, the depth from ocean surface to damaged area must be measured. Then, the pressure on work areas is found by:

$$P = (.445)D$$

where
P = pressure in psi
D = depth of water

The net force on any patch deck or bulkhead is found from the area of the deck or the area of the bulkhead around the flooded compartment. The force is determined by:

$$F = 64(A)(D) \hspace{3cm} \textbf{[7.1]}$$

where
F = force on deck or patch area in pounds
A = area of deck or patch in sq ft
D = depth of water in ft

Example 7-1:

A hole measuring 6 in by 12 in is located 12 ft below the water surface on a sinking ship. (a) What is the water pressure? (b) How much force would be on a mat stuffed over the hole?

Answer:

a) $P = (.445)D$
   $= (.445)(12)$
   $= 5.34$ psi

b) $F = (64)(A)(D)$
   $= (64)(.5)(1)(12)$
   $= 384$ lbs on mat

Since the mat conforms to the hole, the area of the patch is the same as the hole.

The rate at which water will flow through a hole depends upon the size of the hole and its depth below the waterline. The flooding rate is therefore controlled by reducing the hole area, or if possible, by raising the level of the hole. At any point in time, the rate at which the water is flowing through a hole is found by:

$$Q = 3600 \, (A)(\sqrt{D}) \hspace{2cm} [7.2]$$

where
Q = flow rate of water in gallons per minute
A = area of hole in sq ft
D = depth of water above hole in ft

Example 7-2:

At what rate will water flow into the hole of Example 7-1 (a) if the ship were trimmed elevating the hole to 5 ft below the surface? (b) How much difference would that make from 12 ft below? (c) How much force is on the mat at 5 ft?

Answer:

a) $Q = 3600(A)\sqrt{D}$
   $Q_{5ft} = 3600\,(.5)(1)(\sqrt{5})$
   $= 4{,}025$ gpm

b) $Q_{12ft} = 3600(.5)(1)(\sqrt{12})$
   $= 6235$ gpm
   $Q_{12} - Q_5 = 6{,}235 - 4025$
   $= 2{,}210$ gpm

c) $F = 64(A)(D)$
   $= 64(.5)(1)(5)$
   $= 160$ lbs

Tongue and groove wooden planking is a good patching material. To determine the thickness of plank required to patch a hole, the following formula based on fiber stress of 1,000 psi is used:

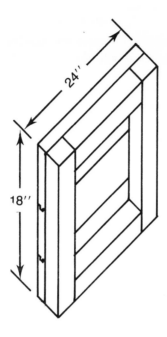

Fig. 7-1. Patch.

$$T = \frac{48(D)(L^2)}{1000} \qquad\qquad \textbf{[7.3]}$$

where
T = plank thickness in inches
D = depth of water to the bottom of the patch in ft
L = length in ft between stiffeners

Example 7-3:
Assuming the depth to the bottom of the patch will be 12 ft, calculate the thickness of plank required to patch the hole in Example 7-1 if stiffeners are placed only around the perimeter of the patch. The patch will measure 24 in x 18 in. Planks will run the long way. (Fig. 7-1)

Answer:
The distance between stiffeners on planks running the long way will be 2 ft.

$$T = \frac{48(12)(4)}{1000}$$
$$= 1.52 \text{ in}$$

Use 1 5/8 in planks

PUMPS

Two applications of pumping concern the diver: pumping to evacuate water from flooded compartments in salvage, and pumping for underwater jetting. Pump terminology must be explained and calculations for pumping operations derived from current standards. Refer to Figure 7-2 for pump terminology. Pumping operations for removing water from a ship require no specific discharge pressures, only volume flow rates. Pumping operations for jetting are concerned with pressure as a main requirement.

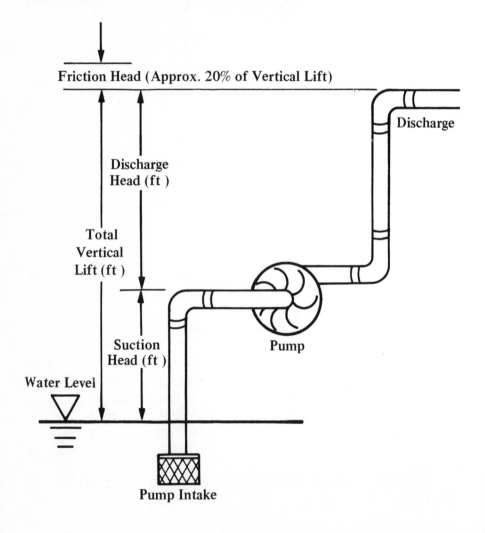

Fig. 7-2. Pump terminology.

Terminology for pumps is based on "dynamic head." The term *head* refers to the pressure exerted by a column of water expressed in feet. A column of water a certain height will exert a specific *pressure* because of its weight. In order to *lift* a column of water a certain *height*, a *suction* head must be applied by the pump to bring the water to the level of the pump. A discharge head above the suction head must be applied to lift the water from the level of the pump to the level of the discharge. Friction in the suction and discharge lines will further increase the entire head required to pump the water. Thus, the total dynamic head of a pump is the sum of the suction and discharge heads (vertical lift in feet) plus an allowance for friction (usually an additional 20%).

To determine the performance of a pump, the suction head is measured in feet. (To provide maximum performance, this distance is kept to a minimum). The total head is then measured (total vertical lift in ft + 20%) and the manufacturer's data will indicate the volume flow rate in gpm that can be expected from the pump at a certain rpm. Representative charts for centrifugal pumps used commonly are given in Figures 7-3, 7-4 and 7-5.

Example 7-4:

How many gpm will the 6 ft centrifugal pump diagramed (Fig. 7-6) deliver?

Answer:

$$\text{Suction head} = 13 \text{ ft}$$
$$\text{Total head} = 12 + 35 + (12 + 35)(.2)$$
$$= 12 + 35 + 9.4$$
$$= 56.4 \text{ ft}$$
Performance from pump, Figure 7-4 = approximately 1,100 gpm

As a flooded compartment is pumped, the water level inside will drop. The suction head, therefore, increases with the corresponding water level decrease reducing pump performance. Since the suction head contributes the most significant reduction in pump performance, the pump should be relocated, if possible, as the water level drops to minimize the suction head. Pumps should also be rigged to change inclination where the pumping operation will tend to change the angle of the ship.

The true test of a diver's patch work will come during pumping operations. As the water is evacuated from behind the patch, the pressure on the patch will increase. Where it is anticipated that a patch will leak, or where patching cannot be complete, the pump must have the additional capacity to keep up with the incoming water besides being able to evacuate the flooded compartment. Estimates of pump capacity requirements can be made by using Equation 7-2 and estimates of the volume of water required to be evacuated from the ship in order to keep her stable.

10″ SALVAGE PUMP

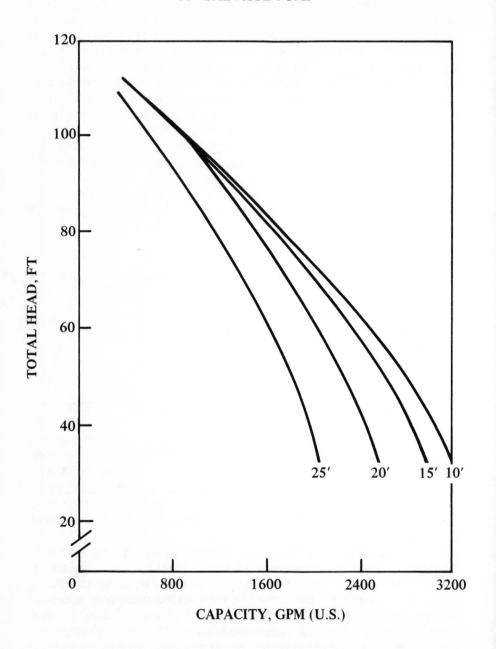

Fig. 7-3. Pump performance for various suction heads.
(Source: *U.S. Navy Salvors Handbook*)

6″ SALVAGE PUMP

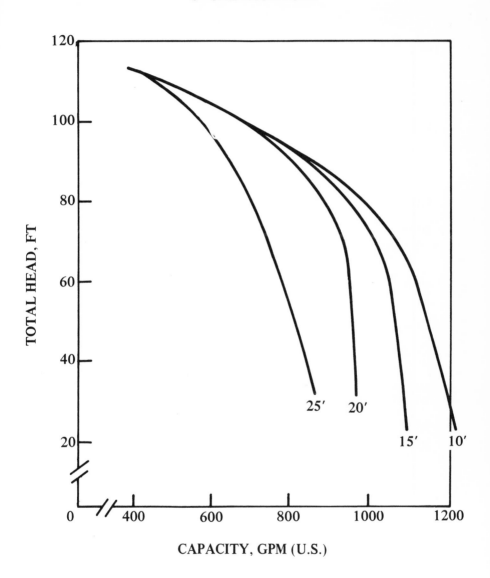

Fig. 7-4. Pump performance for various suction heads.
(Source: *U.S. Navy Salvors Handbook*)

3″ SALVAGE PUMP

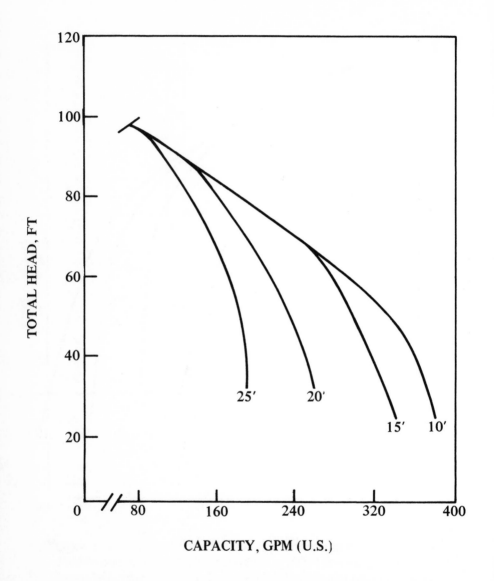

Fig. 7-5. Pump performance for various suction heads.
(Source: *U.S. Navy Salvors Handbook*)

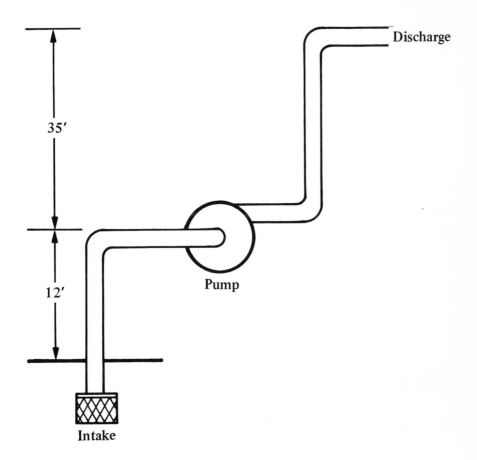

Fig. 7-6. Pumping arrangement for Example 7-4.

Example 7-5:

A grounded tug has taken on an estimated 18,000 gallons of water after tearing several holes in the bottom. You have patched all but a small hole next to a rock where you can't work. The estimated size of the hole is 4 in in diameter and is located 6 ft below the waterline. The tide will be high in 2 hours at which time the tug can be freed *if* you can pump her dry by that time. How many gpm will your pumps have to push?

Answer:

$$\text{Minimum pumping capacity} = \frac{\text{volume to be evacuated}}{\text{time allowed}} + Q_{hole}$$

[7-2]

$$= \frac{18,000}{(60)(2)} + 3600 \left(\pi \left(\frac{2}{12}\right)^2\right) (\sqrt{6})$$

$$= 150 \text{ gpm} + 770 \text{ gpm}$$

$$= 920 \text{ gpm}$$

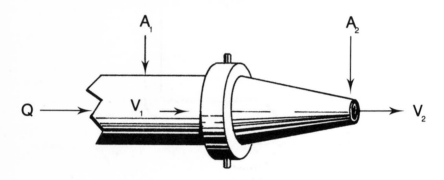

A simple nozzle.

JETTING

Water being pumped through a hose will exert a certain pressure from the water's momentum called the *velocity head*. The velocity head is related to the volume flow rate the pump delivers and the size of the discharge nozzle. For jetting, therefore, we wish to determine this pressure in psi. Since water is virtually incompressible, the water velocity and discharge pressure are predictable by simple mathematics. A fundamental principle of fluid dynamics for incompressible flow in a pipe is that a reduction of cross sectional area (a nozzle) will proportionally increase the water velocity through the nozzle. Thus water velocity in pump hoses and nozzles can be determined:

$$Q = V_1 A_1 = V_2 A_2$$

where

Q = volume flow rate of pump in cu ft per min

V_1 = velocity of water in hose in ft per second

A_1 = cross-sectional area of hose in sq ft

V_2 = velocity at nozzle in fps

A_2 = cross sectional area of nozzle in sq ft

This can be simplified to:

$$V = \frac{Q}{2.4d^2}$$

[7.4]

where
V = velocity in fps at nozzle
Q = pump deliver in gpm
d = diameter of nozzle in inches

The pressure exerted by water being pumped through a hose is:

$$P = 1/2\,\rho V^2$$

where
P   = pressure
ρ = density of fluid

or

$$P = .22V^2$$

[7.5]

for seawater

where
P = water pressure in psi
V = velocity of water in feet per second (from Eq. 7-4)

Example 7-6:
A 3 in centrifugal pump capable of delivering 200 gpm is to be used for jetting. The nozzle used is a balanced type with 1 forward nozzle 1 inch in diameter and 3 opposing nozzles 1 inch in diameter (Fig.7-7). What water pressure will the forward nozzle deliver?

Answer:
An exact evaluation of how much pressure each nozzle exerts would require an analysis of the angle of the opposing nozzles and how their angle affects the pressure. For the purpose of determining the pressure for the jetting nozzle, we can assume that water flows equally out of each nozzle; although it probably flows faster out of the forward nozzle because the water's momentum through the hose is in the forward direction.

Provided each opening is the same size, it is probably a good assumption that water flows equally through each opening. Nozzles used in diving will vary depending upon the application. Keep in mind, therefore, that these equations will be fairly accurate for simple nozzles (one opening) but the more complex angles and openings will not be predicted precisely by these equations. Therefore, if we assume each nozzle takes one-quarter the total volume flow;

$$Q = \frac{200}{4} = 50 \, gpm$$

solving for the velocity at the nozzle,

$$V = \frac{Q}{2.4d^2} = \frac{50}{2.4(1)^2}$$

$$= 21 \, fps$$

the water pressure is therefore

$$P = .22 \, V^2$$
$$= 97 \, psi$$

Keep in mind that water pressure at the nozzle will be hydraulically transmitted through the hose and pump. Therefore, when figuring jetting pressures, use equipment capable of taking the pressure.

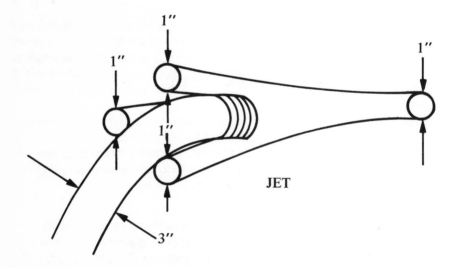

Fig. 7-7. Balanced nozzle.

LOW PRESSURE AIR COMPRESSORS

Some of the most useful tools for underwater work are air powered. Air supply for tools used underwater must meet volume flow and pressure requirements of the tool at the working depth of the dive. The air tool requirements must therefore be adjusted to account for loss of air pressure and volume flow from the effect of water pressure and temperature at the depth of the dive. Air used to refloat or add buoyancy in salvage operations requires careful consideration, not only of the initial volume requirement to attain the desired buoyancy, but also of the pressure and volume changes which occur to the lifting air as the object is raised. The time required to inflate lifting devices to desired buoyancy must often be estimated so that these operations can be controlled as carefully as possible.

Air compressor specifications are denoted by the volume flow capacity at a specified pressure. Displacement cfm for evaluating compressor capacity cannot be used. Displacement cfm does not account for the efficiency of the compressor and therefore does not indicate the actual volume of air delivered by the compressor. The actual volume of air delivered by a compressor (given as cfm of free air) will decrease as the working pressure increases. Air compressors are therefore capable of delivering air at different volume rates and pressures according to the rpm of the compressor.

Generally a compressor is set up to run at a specified rpm and will deliver a certain volume of free air at a specified working pressure which is indicated by the manufacturer.

To arrive at the minimum compressor requirements to run an air powered tool underwater, determine the surface pressure and volume flow requirement for the tool, accounting for the loss of pressure due to friction in the length of hose used (Table 7-1). Then, account for the loss of pressure and volume at the depth of the dive including a factor for temperature effects and add these to the tool requirement.

To account for pressure loss at depth of dive including temperature effects, add

$$P = (.445)D + 50$$

where
P = pressure in psi at working depth
D = depth of dive in feet

to the required working pressure of the tool at the surface. The minimum total working pressure for the tool then becomes

$$P = P_T + (.445)D + 50 \qquad \text{[7.6]}$$

where
P = minimum working pressure in psi
P_T = surface pressure required for tool in psi (including friction)
D = depth in ft

Table 7-1
Approximate Pressure Drop in Air Lines (psi)
Due to Friction Based on 100 psi Working Pressure

Flow in ft³/min	25 ft of 1/2 in hose	50 ft of 1/2 in hose	25 ft of 3/4 in hose	50 ft of 3/4 in hose
20-25	1	1	-	-
25-30	2	2	-	-
30-35	2	4	-	-
35-40	3	5	-	-
40-50	4	8	-	-
50-60	6	12	-	-
60-70	9	18	1	2
70-80	12		2	3
80-90	16		2	3
90-100			3	4
100-120			4	6
120-140			5	8
140-160			7	11
160-180			9	16
180-200			11	

To determine the minimum cfm of free air delivery required by the air compressor, use Boyle's law, and a temperature correction factor;

$$S = \frac{V_T(D + 33)\, T_f}{33}$$

[7.7]

where

S = minimum cfm of free air delivered at the surface to the tool
V_T = surface volume flow required by tool in cfm
D = depth of dive in ft
T_f = temperature correction factor (Table 7-2)

Example 7-7:
An air hammer requiring 45 cfm of free air at 100 psi on the surface is to be operated at a depth of 10 ft below the surface. Water temperature is 40°F. Fifty ft of 1/2 in diameter hose is to be used for the tool. Calculate the compressor requirement.

Table 7-2 Temperature Correction Factor (Tf) for Volume Flow

Water Temperature	30°	50°	70°	100°
Tf	1.2	1.1	1.05	1.0

Answer:

$$S = \frac{V_T(D + 33)T_f}{33}$$

$$= \frac{45(10 + 33)(1.2)}{33}$$

$$= 70.4$$

use at least 71 cfm

$$P = P_T + .445(D) + 50$$

where $P_T = 100 + 18$ (Table 7-1)

use $P_T = 120$ psi

$$= 120 + .445(10) + 50$$
$$= 120 + 4.45 + 50$$
$$= 174.45$$

use 175 psi min working pressure

To estimate the time required to inflate a pontoon, airlift bag or other space used for buoyancy, check first to see that the compressor will deliver at least 50 psi over the bottom pressure:

$$P = .445(D) + 50$$

at least

where
P = working pressure of compressor
D = depth of dive in ft

Then if pressure requirement is met, the approximate time to inflate an air space is estimated by:

$$T = \frac{V_s(D + 33)T_f}{S(33)}$$

[7.8]

(approximately)

where

T = approximate time to inflate in minutes
S = compressor delivery of free air in cfm at surface
V_S = volume of container in cu ft
D = depth in ft
T_f = temperature factor (Table 7-2)

Example 7-8:

Two 1,000 gallon fuel tanks are to be inflated for buoyancy on a ship sunk in 90 ft of water at 50°F. An 80 cfm at 175 psi compressor is to be used. Estimate the time required to inflate both tanks.

Answer:

Pressure check

$$P = (.445)(90) + 50$$
$$= 91 \text{ psi at least}$$

175 psi pressure is OK.

$$V_S = (2000)(.134 \text{ cu ft/gal}) = 268 \text{ ft}^3$$
$$T = \frac{V_S(D + 33)T_f}{S(33)}$$
$$T = \frac{286(90 + 33)1.1}{80(33)}$$

$$= \text{approximately 14 min}$$

More exact calculation of air flow requirements for any purpose can be made by applying the theory of compressible fluid flow. Compressible flow equations account for friction, temperature and depth more precisely than was presented in this Chapter. However, the equations are highly complex and require solution by successive approximations (iterative mathematics) for which a computer is handy. Needless to say, these methods are impractical for working divers.

The methods presented in this Chapter for air flow requirements therefore provide a good guess at best and should not be used if exact air flow requirements need to be determined. For calculation of large volume air flow requirements, or for computing time to inflate large buoyancy compensation compartments, it is recommended that more accurate methods be employed by experts.

SUMMARY OF RELATIONS AND EQUATIONS

Force on patch or submerged bulkhead

$$F = 64 \, (A)(D)$$

where
F = force on bulkhead or patch in pounds
A = area of bulkhead or patch in sq ft
D = depth of water in ft

Rate at which water flows through a hole

$$Q = 3600 \, (A) \, (\sqrt{D})$$

where
Q = flow rate of water in gallons per min
A = area of hole in sq ft
D = depth of water above hole

Thickness of planks to patch hole

$$T = \frac{48(d)(L^2)}{1000}$$

where
T = plank thickness in in
D = depth of water to bottom of patch in ft
L = length in ft between stiffeners

Velocity at jet nozzle

$$V = \frac{Q}{2.4d}$$

where
V = velocity in frs at nozzle
Q = pump delivery in gpm
d = diameter of nozzle in inches

Pressure at jet nozzle

$$P = .22V^2$$

where
P = water pressure at nozzle in psi
V = water velocity at normal in fps

To determine compressor for tools

$$P = P_T + .445 \, (D) + 50$$

where
P   = min working pressure in psi
P_T = surface pressure required for tool in psi including friction
D   = depth of water in ft

$$S = \frac{V_T \, (D+33) T_f}{33}$$

where
S   = min cfm of free air required to run tool at depth
V_T = cfm required to run tool at surface
D   = depth of dive in ft
T_f = temperature factor (Table 7-2)

To estimate time required to inflate air container

$$T = \frac{V_S \, (D+33) T_f}{S(33)} \quad \text{(approximately)}$$

where
T   = approximate time to inflate in min
S   = compressor delivery of free air in cfm at surface
V_S = volume of container in cu ft
D   = depth in ft
T_f = temperature factor

CHAPTER 8: SAFE WORKING LOADS ON RIGGING AND TACKLE

When rigging underwater work, it is necessary to observe standard safety factors. Any rigging job must allow a factor of safety to account for age of materials, friction, bending stress, twisting, sudden jerk, or error in judgement. Therefore, the breaking strength is not used as a value for computing loads on lines and tackle. Breaking strength is divided by a factor of safety to determine the *safe working load*.

FIBER ROPE

Fiber rope is manufactured from either natural plant fibers or synthetic filaments. The natural fiber rope used in the marine environment is primarily manila. Small halyards and tarred twine are made from cotton and jute fibers, but are not used for rigging purposes except for serving splices, seizing and whipping. Synthetic lines are manufactured from nylon, dacron and polypropylene. Each synthetic has its own characteristic advantages or disadvantages depending upon the application (see Table 8-1). Synthetic lines are most widely used because of easier handling, superior strength and easier maintenance.

Table 8-1
Fiber Rope Characteristics

Property	Manila	Nylon	Dacron	Polypropylene
Strength to weight ratio	1	2.84	2.03	2.32
Relative impact resistance	1	8.6	4.0	5.2
Water absorption %	25	4.5	1.5	0
Buoyancy	Sinks	Sinks	Sinks	Floats
Abrasion resistance	Fair	Good	Best	Fair
Mildew resistance	Poor	Excellent	Excellent	Excellent
Acid resistance	Poor	Fair	Good	Excellent
Alkali resistance	Poor	Excellent	Fair	Excellent
Sunlight resistance	Fair	Good	Good	Good
Melting point	Burns	480°F	482°F	330°F

When rope is manufactured from natural fibers, it is not possible to run single fibers the entire length of the rope. Fibers are therefore overlapped and will creep when strained. Some permanent elongation occurs as a result of straining and a continuous load will cause the line to part. Synthetic fibers, on the other hand, can be manufactured in continuous lengths resulting in greater strength and elasticity. Increased elasticity allows the rope to be stretched with

109

less permanent elongation. The restoring force within the stretched rope is a source of potential energy which, when released instantaneously by broken line or slipped knot, will cause the line to snap back with great destructive force.

Rope construction is generally of 3 types; 3 or 4 strand, plaited, or double braided. Three or four strand rope will tend to rotate under loading causing strands to turn back on themselves and the inside yarns to pop through the cover. This is known as *hockling*.

Eight-strand plaited rope has a balanced construction of 4 right- and 4 left-turn strands in pairs. Braided rope also has a balanced construction of right and left running yarns comprising the cover. Both plaited and braided ropes are used for jobs where rotation of lines is a problem. Any time a free end is used, as with an anchor, a balanced construction rope should be employed. Further qualities are tabulated in Table 8-2.

Table 8-2
Qualities of Various Rope Constructions

Quality	Three Strand	Double Braided	Plaited
Breaking strength	Low	High	Medium
Abrasion Resistance	High	Low	Medium
Stretch	High	Low	Highest
Rotation under load	Yes	No	No

The bending radius for all fiber lines should not be less than 3 times its diameter when run through chocks, bitts, bollards, and sheaves. The sheave groove should be about 25% larger than rope diameter. Knots and hitches cause the most severe reductions in strength due to the inherent small bending radius. A small bending radius applied over a prolonged period will crack rope fibers. A splice is therefore more desirable than a knot where applicable (Table 8-3).

When splicing synthetic rope, extra tucks should be made because the line is more slippery than manila. Also remember, that when submerged, water acts to lubricate rope fibers. Therefore, always use extra turns and hitches to insure that the knot will not slip free. Synthetic lines are especially slippery underwater so knots must be tied as tightly as possible with extra hitches. If possible, tuck the free ends in the standing part.

The breaking strength of fiber rope is used as a reference to compute the safe working load. In general, the breaking strength is determined by:

At the Muskegon operation site where the barge *Michigan* is laying intake and discharge pipes for a coal plant on Lake Michigan, the topside preparation of a discharge pipe is shown. Before lowering, turnbuckles are adjusted so that the pipe is level. The pipe is steel with bell and spigot joint and two 0-rings.

Table 8-3 Strength of Knots and Splices

Type	Strength %	Type	Strength %
Overhand knot	45	Short splice	85
Square knot	45	Eye splice with thimble	95
Bowline	60	Long splice	87
Clove hitch	60	Round turn and two half hitches	70

Table 8-4
Weight (lbs per 100 ft) and Breaking Strength (in Tons) of Fiber Rope

Size		Manila		Nylon		Dacron		Polypropylene	
in	cm	w	bs	w	bs	w	bs	w	bs
Diameter:									
1/2	1.27	7.5	1.3	6.1	2.8	7.7	2.5	4.8	1.9
9/16	1.43	10.9	1.7	8.0	3.5	9.5	3.3	6.3	2.4
5/8	1.59	13.3	2.2	10.3	4.2	12.5	4.0	8.3	3.0
3/4	1.91	16.7	2.7	13.9	5.8	16.6	5.5	11.0	3.5
7/8	2.22	22.5	3.9	20.0	8.0	24.2	7.8	15.7	5.5
Circumference:									
3	7.6	27.0	4.5	24.5	11.0	28.5	9.3	19.2	6.5
3 1/4	8.3	31.3	5.3	29.0	13.0	33.5	10.8	22.5	7.4
3 1/2	8.9	36.0	6.0	33.3	14.3	40.0	12.5	26.3	8.3
3 3/4	9.5	41.8	6.8	38.4	16.5	44.0	14.0	30.3	9.8
4	10.2	48.0	7.5	43.5	18.8	50.0	15.5	34.2	10.8
4 1/2	11.4	60.0	9.3	55.5	23.0	63.0	19.5	43.8	13.0
5	12.7	74.4	11.3	66.5	28.5	77.0	24.0	52.5	16.0
5 1/2	14.0	89.5	13.3	80.0	34.0	94.0	28.5	63.2	19.0
6	15.2	108.0	15.5	100.0	40.5	111.0	34.0	79.3	22.0
6 1/2	16.5	125.0	18.0	111.0	45.0	130.0	38.5	91.0	25.0
7	17.8	146.0	20.5	141.0	55.0	152.0	44.0	111.0	30.0
7 1/2	19.1	167.0	23.3	162.0	62.0	175.0	50.0	127.0	34.0
8	20.3	191.0	26.0	182.0	68.5	200.0	55.0	142.0	37.5
9	22.9	242.0	32.0	232.0	85.0	250.0	70.0	183.0	47.0
10	25.4	299.0	38.5	294.0	100.0	303.0	82.5	232.0	57.5
11	28.0	367.0	45.5	350.0	120.0	375.0	100.0	272.0	69.0
12	30.5	436.0	52.5	416.0	140.0	445.0	115.0	325.0	82.0

(Source: *U.S. Navy Salvors Handbook*)

Table 8-5 Factor of Safety

Rope	Standing Rigging	Running Rigging
Manila	5	7
Polypropylene	6	8
Dacron	6	12
Nylon	9	12

(Source: *U.S. Navy Salvors Handbook*)

$$BS = C^2(900) \text{ for manila} \qquad \textbf{[8.1]}$$

$$BS = C^2(2400) \text{ for synthetics} \qquad \textbf{[8.2]}$$

where
BS = breaking strength in lbs
C = rope circumference in inches

Table 8-4 gives the specific minimum breaking strengths for new, clean, dry fiber rope. To compute the safe working load on fiber rope, the breaking strength must be divided by a factor of safety (Table 8-5).

$$SWL = \frac{BS}{F} \qquad \textbf{[8.3]}$$

where
SWL = safe working load in lbs
BS = breaking strength in lbs from Equations 8-1, 8-2, or Table 8-4
F   = factor of safety from Table 8-5

Where synthetic rope is substituted for manila, the substitution size of synthetic rope should be size for size for lines up to 3 inches in circumference. For larger lines, Equation 8.4 or Table 8-6 should be used to determine the

Table 8-6 Substitute Synthetic Size for Manila

Manila	Nylon	Dacron	Polyproplylene
3	2 3/4	2 3/4	2 3/4
3 1/4	2 3/4	2 3/4	3
3 1/2	2 3/4	2 3/4	3
3 3/4	3	3	3 1/4
4	3 1/4	3 1/4	3 1/2
4 1/2	3 1/2	3 1/2	4
5	4	4	4 1/2
5 1/2	4 1/2	4 1/2	5
6	4 1/2	5	5 1/2
6 1/2	5	5	5 1/2
7	5 1/2	5 1/2	6
7 1/2	6	6	6 1/2
8	6	6 1/2	7
8 1/2	6 1/2	6 1/2	7 1/2
9	7	7	8
10	7 1/2	8	8 1/2
11	8 1/2	8 1/2	9 1/2
12	9	9	10

Notes:
- All sizes are circumference in inches.
- All ropes three strand construction.
- Under 3 in substitute size for size.

(Source: *U.S. Navy Salvors Handbook*)

Table 8-7 Nominal Breaking Strength of Galvanized Wire Rope

Rope Diameter		Approx. Weight lbs/ft		Breaking Strength in Tons					
				6 x 19 class			6 x 37 class		
				Improved P/S		Extra Improved P/S	Improved P/S		Extra Improved P/S
in	mm	fiber core	IWRC	fiber core	IWRC	IWRC	fiber core	IWRC	IWRC
1/4	6.33	.105	.116	2.47	2.67	3.06	2.33	2.67	2.88
5/16	7.92	.164	.180	3.88	4.12	4.74	3.63	3.90	4.48
3/8	9.51	.236	.260	5.49	5.90	6.80	5.19	5.58	6.43
7/16	11.11	.32	.35	7.44	8.00	9.18	7.04	7.57	8.70
1/2	12.70	.42	.46	9.63	10.4	12.0	9.18	9.90	11.3
9/16	14.28	.53	.59	12.2	12.1	15.1	11.6	12.5	14.3
5/8	15.87	.66	.72	15.0	16.1	18.5	14.2	15.3	17.6
3/4	19.05	.95	1.04	21.4	23.0	26.5	20.3	21.9	25.1
7/8	22.23	1.29	1.42	29.0	31.1	35.8	27.5	29.6	34.0
1	25.40	1.68	1.85	37.6	40.4	46.5	33.6	35.8	44.2
1 1/8	28.58	2.13	2.34	47.3	50.8	58.5	45.1	48.5	55.7
1 1/4	31.75	2.63	2.89	58.1	62.5	71.9	55.4	59.4	68.5
1 3/8	34.93	3.18	3.50	69.9	75.2	86.4	66.7	71.7	82.5
1 1/2	38.10	3.78	4.16	82.8	89.0	102.6	79.1	85.1	97.2
1 5/8	41.28	4.44	4.88	96.3	103.5	118.8	92.7	99.9	114.0
1 3/4	44.45	5.15	5.67	111.6	119.7	137.7	107.0	115.0	131.0
1 7/8	47.63	5.91	6.50	126.9	136.8	156.6	122.0	131.0	151.0
2	50.80	6.72	7.39	144.0	154.8	178.2	139.0	149.0	171.0
2 1/8	53.98	7.59	8.35	161.1	172.8	198.9	156.0	167.0	193.0
2 1/4	57.15	8.51	9.36	180.0	193.5	222.3	174.0	186.0	215.0
2 3/8	60.33	9.48	10.4	199.8	215.0	246.6	193.0	207.0	238.0
2 1/2	63.50	10.5	11.6	220.0	235.0	272.0	212.0	229.0	263.0
2 5/8	66.68	11.6	12.8	240.0	259.0	298.0	234.0	251.0	289.0
2 3/4	69.85	12.7	14.0	263.0	283.0	325.0	256.0	275.0	315.0

(Source: U.S. Navy Salvors Handbook)

substitute size. While it is true that, size for size, synthetic line is stronger than manila, the criteria for substitution must account for strength loss from cuts as well as abrasion during use. Therefore, it is dangerous to use a smaller size synthetic line in replacement of manila (unless using Equation 8.4 for lines over 3 inches in circumference) because smaller synthetic line suffers greater loss of strength from small cuts and abrasion.

Replacement = same size as manila up to 3 in circumference
Synthetic Size
(circumference) = $\sqrt{0.6S^2 + 0.4\,M^2}$ **[8.4]**

where
S = size (circumference) of synthetic rope with equal or greater breaking strength of manila in use
M = size (circumference) of manila in use in inches

Example 8-1:
Manila line in use with a circumference of 6 inches must be replaced with nylon line. Using Equations 8.1, 8.2, and 8.4, calculate the size of nylon line required.
Answer:

$$\text{size} = \sqrt{0.6(S^2) + 0.4(M)^2}$$
$$M = 6$$

To find S

$$BS_{manila} = BS_{nylon}$$
$$M^2(900) = S^2(2400)$$
$$(36)(900) = S^2(2400)$$
$$S^2 = 13.5$$
$$\text{Replacement} = \sqrt{(.6)(13.5) + (.4)(36)}$$
$$= \sqrt{22.5}$$
$$= 4.74$$

Use 4-3/4 in circumference nylon to replace 6 in circumference manila

WIRE ROPE

Wire rope for marine use is generally constructed from improved plow steel or extra improved plow steel and has either a fiber core or an independent wire rope core (IWRC). Other metals and cores are used along with special construction techniques for a variety of applications. However, the use of such special materials and techniques is directed by wire rope engineers and is beyond the scope of this chapter.

Wire rope is measured by diameter and is designated by 2 numbers. The first number in each class represents the number of strands in the wire. The second number represents the lower limit of the number of wires per strand. Table 8-7 is a partial list of wire rope classes and some of their properties. Generally, wire rope with more strands or more wires per strand has better flexibility. Wire rope with fewer strands or wires increases resistance to abrasion. Where compression or heat resistance are required, an independent wire rope core (IWRC) should be used instead of the fiber core. Flexibility and handling ease will be diminished by using the IWRC.

Breaking strength of wire rope can be approximated by the relation

$$BS = C^2(8,000) \qquad \textbf{[8.5]}$$

where
BS = breaking strength of wire rope in lbs
C = wire circumference in inches

To determine the safe working load for wire rope use the factor of safety from Table 8-8.

Table 8-8 Factor of Safety for Wire Rope

Condition	Factor of Safety
New perfect condition standing rigging	5
New perfect condition running rigging	10
Used good condition standing rigging	6
Used good condition running rigging	12

CHAIN

Chain is usually either open link, stud link, or dielock type construction. The latter two types have a stiffener or stud in the link to prevent the link from collapsing under load and also to prevent the chain from tangling. The stud link type chain is often used in salvage and marine practice.

Chain is measured according to the bar stock diameter used in manufacturing the links. The length of chain is expressed in *shots*. A shot of chain equals 15 fathoms or 90 feet.

The strength of chain is expressed by the break test load in pounds. The break test load is applied by the manufacturer at regular intervals to establish the ultimate strength of the chain. To determine the safe working load of chain, consult the manufacturer's specification for the working load limit. The safe working load for chain is sometimes calculated at one-quarter the break test load for gradual straight line load. Tables for some chain are given in Table 8-9.

SHACKLES, HOOKS AND TURNBUCKLES

The safe working load on a shackle can be calculated by using the formula:

Table 8-9 Chain; Weight Per Shot and Break Test

		High Strength		Die-lock	Superstrength Die-lock	
size		weight per shot	break test tons	break test tons	weight per shot	break test tons
in	mm	lb	(2000 lbs)	(2000 lbs)	lb	(2000 lbs)
3/4	19.1	505	24	38	630	46
1	25.4	909	42	64	1,125	79
1 1/4	31.8	1,415	65	99	1,770	122
1 1/2	38.1	2,035	93	140	2,505	172
1 3/4	44.5	2,720	125	190	3,400	232
2	40.8	3,525	161	244	4,400	298
2 1/4	57.2	4,460	202	305	5,560	372
2 1/2	63.5	5,528	246	372	6,900	454
2 3/4	69.9	6,725	294	442	8,400	540
3	76.2	8,035	347	522	10,050	637
3 1/4	82.6	9,460	402	605	11,825	738
3 1/2	88.9	10,998	461	692	13,700	844
3 3/4	95.3	12,626	523	875	15,800	1,068
4	101.6	14,100	588	998	17,600	1,218

(Source: *U.S. Navy Salvors Handbook*)

$$SWL = 3(D^2) \tag{8.6}$$

where
SWL = safe working load in tons
D   = diameter of shackle bow (Fig. 8-1)

A hook is the weakest part of a tackle (Fig. 8-1) with a safe working load

$$SWL = 2/3 \, D^2 \tag{8.7}$$

where
SWL = safe working load (ton)
D   = diameter of hook at shank

Turnbuckles are measured by the diameter of the threaded stock and the distance inside the barrel. The safe working load on turnbuckles is computed by

$$SWL = 4(D^2) \tag{8.8}$$

where
SWL = safe working load in tons (safety factor of 5)
D   = diameter of threaded part in inches

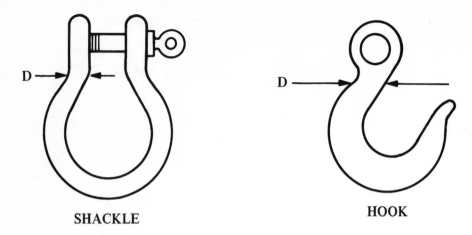

SHACKLE

HOOK

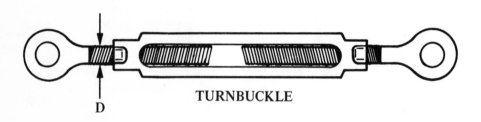

TURNBUCKLE

Fig. 8-1. Tackle.

PURCHASES

Lines and pulleys used to gain mechanical advantage when hoisting or pulling heavy objects are called purchases. Generally one block is secured to a stationary fitting and is known as the *standing* block. The other block is secured to the object to be lifted or hauled and is the *running* block. The line passed to the winch is the *hauling part*. The line or lines between the blocks are called the *fall*.

A single block and tackle (Fig. 8-2) consists of one block and a hauling line. A multiple or *luff* tackle consists of two blocks with one or more sheaves in each block. The theoretical mechanical advantage gained by using an arrangement of blocks and tackle is equal to the number of parts at the running block (Fig. 8-2). The actual mechanical advantage depends upon the friction in the blocks. Allowing for friction, the pull necessary to lift a known weight with a purchase can be determined by:

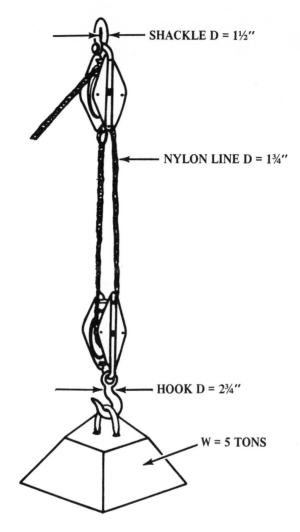

Fig. 8-2. Single luff purchase.

$$P = \frac{W + [(0.1)W(N)]}{MA}$$

[8.9]

where
P = necessary pulling force
W = load weight
N = number of sheaves
MA = mechanical advantage of purchase

The safe working load on a purchase allowing for sheave friction can be determined by

$$SWL = \frac{10(MA)(SWL_{line})}{10 + N}$$

[8.10]

where
SWL   = safe working load of purchase in tons
MA   = mechanical advantage of purchase
SWL_{line} = safe working load in tons of the line reeved in the purchase
N   = number of sheaves in system

Example 8-2:

The block and tackle system shown (Fig. 8-2) is to lift a five ton weight. Is it safe? If so, how much pull is required?

Answer:

1. check shackle

$$SWL = 3(D^2)$$
$$= 6.75 \text{ tons}$$

OK

2. check hook

$$SWL = 2/3(D^2)$$
$$= 5 \text{ tons}$$

OK, but mouse it

3. check purchase

$$SWL = \frac{10(MA)(SWL_{line})}{(10 + N)}$$

$$MA = 2$$

$$SWL_{line} = \frac{C^2(2400)}{8}$$

$$= 8,269 \text{ lbs}$$
$$= 4.1 \text{ tons}$$
$$N = 2$$

$$SWL = \frac{10(2)(4.1)}{(10 + 2)}$$

$$= 6.7 \text{ tons}$$

OK

4. pull required

$$P = \frac{W + [(0.1)WN]}{MA}$$

$$= \frac{5 + (0.1)(5)(2)}{2}$$

$$= 3 \text{ tons}$$

SUMMARY OF RELATIONS AND EQUATIONS

Breaking strength of fiber line

$$BS = C^2(900) \text{ manila}$$
$$BS = C^2(2400) \text{ synthetic}$$

where BS = breaking strength in pounds

Safe working load on fiber line

$$SWL = \frac{BS}{F}$$

where
SWL = safe working load in pounds
BS = breaking strength in pounds
F = factor of safety (Table 8-5)

Replacement of synthetic line for manila

Replacement = size for size up to 3 inches circumference
Size
$$(\text{Circumference}) = \sqrt{0.6\,S^2 + 0.4\,M^2}$$

where
S = circumference in inches of synthetic rope with equal or greater breaking strength to manila in use
M = circumference of manila in use in inches

Breaking strength of wire rope

$$BS = C^2(8,000)$$

where
BS = breaking strength in lbs
C = wire circumference in inches

Safe working load of wire rope

$$SWL = \frac{BS}{F}$$

where
SWL = safe working load in lbs
BS = breaking strength in lbs
F = factor of safety (Table 8-8)

Safe working load on shackle

$$SWL = 3\,D^2$$

where
SWL = safe working load in tons
D   = diameter of shackle at bow

Safe working load on hook

$$SWL = 2/3D^2$$

where
SWL = safe working load in tons
D   = diameter of hook at shank

Safe working load on turnbuckle

$$SWL = 4 D^2$$

where
SWL = safe working load in tons
D   = diameter of threaded part in inches

Pull required on purchase

$$P = \frac{W + [0.1(W)(N)]}{MA}$$

where
P   = necessary pulling force
W   = load weight
N   = number of sheaves
MA   = mechanical advantage of purchase

Safe working load on purchase

$$SWL = \frac{10(MA)(SWL_{line})}{10 + N}$$

where
SWL   = safe working load of purchase in tons
MA   = mechanical advantage of purchase
N   = number of sheaves in system
SWL_{line} = safe working load in tons of line received in purchase

CHAPTER 9: CORROSION OF MATERIALS

Because of the highly corrosive nature of the marine environment, it is necessary for the working diver to have an understanding of the processes of corrosion and other destructive forces which he will encounter underwater. With proper understanding, an intelligent selection of materials can be made with regard to *cost* and *durability*. Complex problems of corrosion and deterioration require analysis by materials experts. However, a great deal of "foolish" corrosion can be prevented by applying fundamental principles presented here. This chapter is not intended for use in design, but rather for applying some common sense to corrosion detection and prevention underwater.

CORROSION

Corrosion refers to the destructive process imposed upon metals when they are exposed to a solution capable of conducting an electric current (an electrolyte). Although several types of corrosion are found in the marine environment, the basic corrosion process is created by the flow of electricity between certain areas of a metal surface through seawater.

The electric current which causes corrosion is very small, and is caused either by the potential of a metal to change from a refined form into its natural state or the potential of two dissimilar metals to create an electric current (galvanic potential).

For this electrochemical reaction (corrosion) to occur, four factors are required to be present at the same time: Anode, Cathode, Electrolyte, and electrical contact between anode and cathode.

- The *Anode* is the metal area where the electric current leaves the metal and enters the electrolytic solution. The anode is destructively altered or eaten away by the corrosion process.
- The *Cathode* is the metal area where the electrons released by the anode are used to give off negatively charged ions into the electrolytic solution or combine with positive ions from solution. Little or no metal damage occurs at the cathode area.
- The *Electrolyte* is the solution capable of conducting an electric current which, for the working diver, is seawater and also some polluted waters.
- *Electrical contact* between cathode and anode is formed by metal to metal contact or by wire. The anode and cathode can occur on the same metal surface (as we shall see in the case of pitting), in which case contact is inevitable. Or, they may be different metals in which case contact must be made for corrosion to occur.

If any one of the foregoing conditions is not present simultaneously with the other three, corrosion is halted.

TYPES OF CORROSION

In the marine environment, several types of corrosion commonly occur and are of concern to the diver for various reasons. Inspection diving requires a knowledge of all types of corrosion and the resulting deterioration which may occur. Construction diving necessitates an understanding of potential corrosion problems and how to avoid them.

Table 9-1 Tolerance for Crevices Immersed in Quiet Seawater

Useful Resistance				Not Resistant
Highest	Good	Fair	Less	
Nickel-chromium high molybdenum alloys Titanium (Susceptible in hot seawater)	90/10 copper-nickel alloy (1.5 Fe) 70/30 copper-nickel alloy (0.5 Fe) Bronze, Brass Austenitic nickel cast iron	Nickel-iron-chromium 825	Nickel-copper alloy 400	Type 316 Nickel-chromium Type 304 Type 400 series

(Source: International Nickel Company, Inc.)

General corrosion (Fig. 9-1) occurs over the entire exposed surface of a metal. The anodes and cathodes are not stable on the surface in this case and shift continuously. Corrosion is, therefore, uniform over the entire surface and in some instances may form a protective film which inhibits further corrosion. Many times, general corrosion occurs in air more readily than underwater. The splash zone, above the high tide level, creates favorable conditions for general corrosion especially for iron and steel (widely used materials in marine construction).

Pitting (Fig. 9-2) is a form of localized attack especially common on important structural alloys (an alloy is a combination of two or more metals or a metal and nonmetal which are intimately mixed by fusion to form a new substance with altered properties of strength, hardness and corrosion resistance). Steel alloys and aluminum alloys are two commonly used materials in the marine environment and are susceptible to attack by pitting. Pitting occurs when an area on the metal surface begins to act as an anode. The area acting as the anode starts to corrode while the rest of the metal surface acts as a cathode and does not corrode, a situation which occurs in general corrosion, except that anode and cathode areas formed by general corrosion continuously shift allowing a uniform pattern of corrosion to occur on the metal surface. In the case of pitting, however, the areas which begin to act as anodes continue to do so, and thus form pits instead of a uniform layer of corrosion.

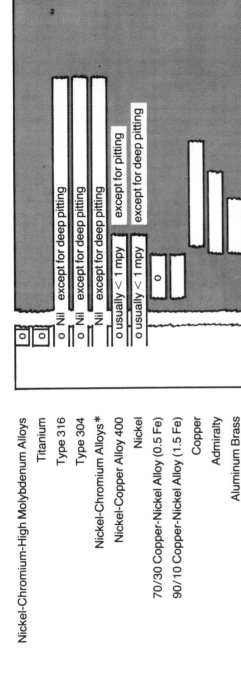

Nickel-Chromium-High Molybdenum Alloys

Titanium

Type 316

Type 304

Nickel-Chromium Alloys*

Nickel-Copper Alloy 400

Nickel

70/30 Copper-Nickel Alloy (0.5 Fe)

90/10 Copper-Nickel Alloy (1.5 Fe)

Copper

Admiralty

Aluminum Brass

G Bronze

Nickel-Aluminum Bronze

Nickel-Aluminum-Manganese Bronze

Manganese Bronze

Austenitic Nickel Cast Iron

Carbon Steel

Typical Average Corrosion Rates Mils per Year
(1 mil = .001 inch)

Nil   0.1   0.5   1   2   5   10

o Data from results of early tests at depths of 2300 to 5600 feet.

* Nickel-chromium alloys designate a family of nickel base alloys with sub-
stantial chromium contents with or without other alloying elements all of
which, except those with high molybdenum contents, have related seawater corrosion characteristics.

Fig. 9-1. General corrosion.
(Source: International Nickel Company, Inc.)

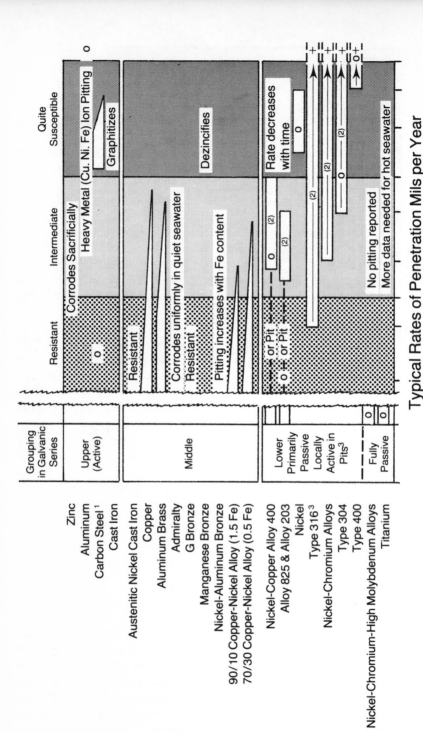

Fig. 9-2. Pitting.
(Source: International Nickel Company, Inc.)

Typical Rates of Penetration Mils per Year

Crevice corrosion (Table 9-1)—as stated, some metals will form a thin layer of corrosion which can act as a protective film. Many of the useful metals and alloys for marine service are corrosion resistant because they form an extremely thin adherent oxide film which protects the underlying metal from attack by seawater. However, the film is under constant attack by various forces which try to break down its protective qualities. The only reason the film is so useful is that it will self-repair any intrusion as long as oxygen is available to form a new film. (Seawater does contain dissolved oxygen.) A problem arises in crevice areas such as slightly open joints, under bolt heads, nuts, washers, and even under barnacles where there is limited oxygen available for the metal to repair its protective film. In such areas, a localized attack called crevice corrosion occurs. The area of metal in the crevice will act as an anode while the area of metal protected by the film will act as a cathode as long as the water is relatively still.

In moving seawater certain alloys, which pit and undergo crevice corrosion in quiet seawater, will cease corrosion because the oxygen needed for self repair becomes available by the moving water rushing in and out of pits and crevices. As water speed increases, however, other forms of corrosion will take place.

Erosion corrosion is due to the velocity of water. Most commonly it occurs at elbows and T-joints inside pipes especially in seawater cooling systems. Some metals, such as iron, will be affected by any increase in water velocity because the semi-protective oxide film will be removed. Other metals will experience a breakdown of protective oxide films at a certain velocity (called critical velocity) where the adhering strength of the film to the metal is overcome by the rapidly flowing water.

Cavitation corrosion (Table 9-2) is also caused by the velocity of water, but it differs from erosion corrosion because the mechanism of attack is different. The most common and troublesome occurrence of cavitation corrosion is on propeller blades which will be used here to illustrate the mechanism of cavitation corrosion.

As a propeller spins through water at high speed, the pressure on the leading side of the blade increases. The back side of the blade has a corresponding pressure drop. When the pressure drops below a certain level, water vapor bubbles are formed (similar to the bubbles of boiling water) at the surface of the blade. When the bubbles collapse, water will rush in to fill the void and strike the blade surface. The assault caused by water striking the blade in this manner will either physically gouge the metal or at least break through the protective film. The attack will often continue repeatedly in the same area because of the symmetry of the propeller. Over a period of time, considerable damage can be done and once any damage to the smooth surface of the blade begins, the roughness accelerates the process.

Galvanic corrosion (Fig. 9-3) is probably the most common kind of "foolish" corrosion which occurs underwater. Anytime two dissimilar metals are in

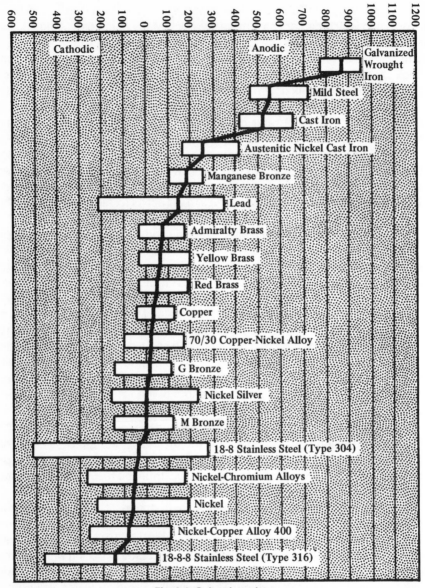

Fig. 9-3. Galvanic series.
(Source: International Nickel Company, Inc.)

contact underwater, they form a small battery (galvanic cell) which conducts electricity through the seawater. The two dissimilar metals form an electric potential which causes electrons to flow from the metal acting as an anode to the metal acting as a cathode thus causing one metal (the anode) to corrode

Table 9-2
Order of Resistance to Cavitation Damage in Seawater

Resistance to Cavitation Damage Rating	Metals
Group I—Most Resistant. Little or no damage. Useful under supercavitating conditions.	Cobalt base hard facing alloy Titanium alloys Austenitic (Series 300) and precipitation hardened stainless steels Nickel-chromium alloys such as alloy 625 and alloy 718 Nickel-molybdenum-chromium alloy C
Group II—These metals are commonly utilized where a high order of resistance to cavitation damage is required but are subject to some metal loss under the most severe conditions of cavitation.	Nickel-copper-aluminum alloy K-500 Nickel-copper alloy 400 Nickel-aluminum bronze Nickel-aluminum-manganese bronze
Group III—These metals have some degree of cavitation resistance but are generally limited to low speed low performance type applications	70/30 copper-nickel alloy Manganese bronze G Bronze and M Bronze Sustenitic nickel cast irons
Group IV—These metals are normally not used in applications where cavitation damage may occur unless heavily protected.	Carbon and low alloy steels Cast irons Aluminum and aluminum alloys

(Source: International Nickel Company, Inc.)

more rapidly and the other (cathode) to corrode more slowly or even cease corroding altogether. Metals and alloys are classified according to their electromotive potential or their "nobility" in the galvanic series. The more noble metals are the most cathodic or have the higher potential to receive electrons. The less noble metal (or more active) will always give up electrons, or dissolve, and become the anode of the corrosion cell. Any time two dissimilar metals are in contact underwater, the anode will dissolve at a rate which depends on how different the metals are on the galvanic chart. Sometimes, the process of galvanic corrosion is felt by the diver. The slight electric current in the water will cause dental fillings to "tingle," and a sour taste in the mouth results. The tingling caused by *electrolysis* will be discussed later.

De-alloying corrosion (Table 9-3) occurs when one of the elements of a metal's alloys is selectively attacked. Without changing the outward shape of the metal, the more active element usually escapes, leaving with the alloy the more noble element. What occurs precisely is unknown, but the remanent metal is usually porous and soft and has greatly reduced strength. Brass

At Jamestown Bridge in Jamestown, Rhode Island, diver is about to clean and inspect a pier. Underwater damage was so severe from erosion that the entire footing had to be rebuilt. Diver wears a unisuit and Kirby-Morgan KM B-9 mask. A tender assists.

containing more than 15% zinc is subject to "dezincification" by this type of corrosion. The remanent of dezincification is a spongy red copper. Often de-alloying corrosion will go undetected because the general appearance of the affected metal is unchanged.

Stress corrosion (Fig. 9-4) cracking occurs as a result of the combined action of mechanical stress and exposure to corrosion. Mechanical stress may result from such causes as service loads, bolting, and welding. This type of corrosion is not necessarily a slow process and may occur over a period of hours with some high strength steels, such as stainless steel and maraging steel. (Maraging steel families are the result of recent metalurgical improvements in reducing impurities such as phosphorus, sulfur, oxygen, and nitro-

Table 9-3
Selective Corrosion

	Susceptible	Solutions
Graphitization	Cast iron Ductile	Use austenitic nickel cast iron
Dezincification	Copper alloys with more than 14% Zn. Examples: naval brass, admiralty, aluminum brass, muntz metal, manganese, bronze	1. Use inhibited grade 2. Use alloys with less than 15% Zn. Examples: red brass, silicon bronze, tin bronze, copper-nickels
Dealuminification	Aluminum bronzes with less than 4% Ni	Use 4% Ni grade
Denickelification	70/30 copper nickel refinery condenser at high temperature and low flow	Don't run condenser dry. Keep 3 ft per sec min flow.
Intergranular Erosion of Austenitic Stainless Steel	Heat of welding or slow cooling of castings low to selective attack of stainless steel in seawater but has little effect in marine atmosphere	1. Anneal 2. Use low carbon grades—304L,316L,CF-4M 3. Use stabilized grade 347 or 321 4. Avoid welding after annealing of susceptible grades

(Source: International Nickel Company, Inc.)

gen, the result being steels with yield strengths between 150,000 to 300,000 psi which are ductile and can be heat treated to be less brittle.) Corrosion fatigue is a similar type of stress corrosion except that the loading on fatigue failure is intermittent rather than sustained. Also related to stress corrosion cracking is *hydrogen embrittlement*. The attack is due to atomic hydrogen penetrating the metal and combining either with the metal or with another hydrogen atom to form a hydrogen molecule. The result is a high internal pressure which cracks the metal. The hydrogen atoms can be produced by the corrosion of steel or by a cathodic protection system which will be discussed later.

ELECTROLYSIS

Although not considered an actual corrosion process, metal deterioration can be rapid and severe when electrolysis does occur. This is a principle

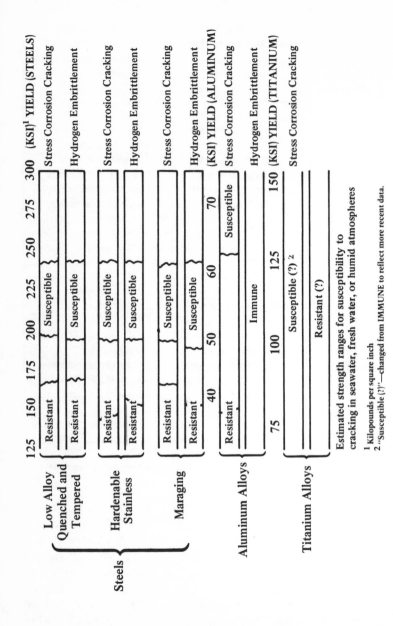

Fig. 9-4. Stress corrosion.
(Source: International Nickel Company, Inc.)

132

similar to galvanic corrosion except that dissimilar metals are activated by an *induced* electric field rather than by their own galvanic potential. The resulting deterioration of the metals is not corrosion per se, but because the deterioration is induced by a local electrical field, it is termed "electrolysis." A battery improperly grounded in a boat may cause the fastenings to dissolve by electrolysis.

FOULING (TABLE 9-4)

Marine fouling refers to the attachment and growth of marine organisms to surfaces which result in loss of operational efficiency or deterioration of the surface. The problem remains largely unsolved. Barnacle scraping and painting of surfaces seems to be the time honored solution although some discrimination in use of materials can be effective (Table 9-4). Copper paints are helpful in slowing the attachment and growth of fouling organisms.

CORROSION PREVENTION

The three common methods of corrosion prevention for the underwater environment are by material selection, painting or coating, and cathodic protection. As already mentioned, the basis behind corrosion prevention is eliminating one of the four factors necessary to sustain the corrosion process. The diver need not concern himself with design considerations underwater. Design problems are complex and must account at once for all the variables including temperature and velocity of water. These complicated issues are best left to experts. However, knowing the causes of corrosion and the fundamentals of prevention can contribute to better inspection efforts and better construction techniques.

Material Selection (Fig. 9-5):

For the purpose of selecting materials for underwater use, where necessary, a series of charts and tables are included in this chapter. These illustrate graphically the variety of considerations involved in proper selection. However, some general conclusions about marine materials should always be remembered.

1. Wherever possible, construct equipment for seawater use from *one* metal or alloy. Select this metal or alloy for its corrosion resistance. For example, do not use iron nails to fasten copper sheathing. Use copper nails to fasten copper sheathing.
2. Where it is not possible to construct from only one metal or alloy, isolate the different metals if feasible, always making certain the *key* components are more noble (protected).
3. Expect and allow for increased corrosion on the less noble metal

Table 9-4
Fouling Resistance—Quiet Seawater

Materials	Arbitrary Rating Scale of Fouling Resistance	
Copper 90/100 copper-nickel alloy	90-100	Best
Brass and bronze	70-90	Good
70/30 copper-nickel alloy, aluminum bronze, zinc	50	Fair
Nickel-copper alloy 400	10	Very Slight
Carbon and low alloy steels, stainless steels, Nickel-chromium-high molybdenum alloys Titanium	0	Least

(Source: International Nickel Company, Inc.)

(anode) by providing a large area or heavy wall to support the increased corrosion that will occur.
4. Where safety is a factor and there is any question, consult an expert.

Painting and Coating:

Painting is the most common corrosion control method. Recently coatings or long life paints, such as vinyl and epoxy, have been used effectively in the marine environment. Coatings are more expensive than conventional paints, and therefore, surface preparation is of prime importance for the durability of these coatings. If good surface preparation is assured, use a coating for longer lasting cover before immersion. If, there is a poor surface, paint should be applied. The diver is more often involved in maintenance, in which case the surface is probably already somewhat corroded and paint should be used. It is important to consider the galvanic effect carefully before painting cast iron or steel. If either is in contact with a more noble metal, it is often better to paint the more noble metal and leave the steel bare. This is the opposite of conventional practice.

FASTENER

BASE METAL	Aluminum [1]	Carbon Steel	Silicon Bronze	Nickel	Nickel-Chromium Alloys	Type 304	Nickel-Copper Alloy 400	Type 316
Aluminum	Neutral	Comp. [2]	Unsatis- [2] factory	Comp. [2]	Comp.	Comp.	Comp. [2]	Comp.
Steel and Cast Iron	N.C.	Neutral	Comp.	Comp.	Comp.	Comp.	Comp.	Comp.
Austenitic Nickel Cast Iron	N.C.	N.C.	Comp.	Comp.	Comp.	Comp.	Comp.	Comp.
Copper	N.C.	N.C.	Comp.	Comp.	Comp.	Comp.	Comp.	Comp.
70/30 Copper-Nickel Alloy	N.C.	N.C.	N.C.	Comp.	Comp.	Comp.	Comp.	Comp.
Nickel	N.C.	N.C.	N.C.	Neutral	Comp. [3]	Comp. [3]	Comp.	Comp. [3]
Type 304	N.C.	N.C.	N.C.	N.C.	May [4] Vary	Neutral [3]	Comp.	Comp. [4]
Nickel-Copper Alloy 400	N.C.	N.C.	N.C.	N.C.	May [4] Vary	May [4] Vary	Neutral	May [4] Vary
Type 316	N.C.	N.C.	N.C.	N.C.	May [4] Vary	May [4] Vary	May [4] Vary	Neutral [4]

(1) Anodizing would change ratings as fastener.
(2) Fasteners are compatible and protected but may lead to enlargement of bolt hold in aluminum plate.
(3) Cathodic protection afforded fastener by the base metal may not be enough to prevent crevice corrosion of fastener particularly under head of bolt fasteners.
(4) May suffer crevice corrosion, under head of bolt fasteners.

NOTE: Comp. = Compatible, Protected.   N.C. = Not Compatible, Preferentially Corroded.

Fig. 9-5. Galvanic compatibility (seawater fasteners).
(Source: International Nickel Company, Inc.)

Cathodic Protection:

Most working divers are familiar with cathodic protection systems. One type is commonly found on ship's hulls (called zincs). This type of protection is of use only on submerged metals and alloys. It is not used above water. Proper painting in conjunction with cathodic protection provides the most effective corrosion control method.

Cathodic protection is either impressed or galvanic, an impressed system which uses an external power source (electrolysis controlled to protect key components). Galvanic protection sacrifices an active metal (zinc, magnesium or aluminum) which is attached to the preferred metal underwater. Since the preferred metal receives electrons from the zinc, it becomes a cathode. When a metal becomes a cathode, it can no longer readily corrode. Most metals underwater can be protected in this manner. When used with the proper paint, the sacrificial anode protects holes in the paint. At the stern of a ship, zincs reduce or eliminate the galvanic effect of the propeller.

CHAPTER 10: COMPASS CALCULATIONS

A good compass can be a valuable asset to the working diver if he understands how to use it and under what circumstances it can be relied upon. Indeed, there are many situations where proper use of a compass underwater will be indispensable. But, the compass does have severe limitations which must be kept in mind.

Since most of the diver's attention is on the compass and not on the search, use of a compass in search is often thought of as wasteful. However, there are occasions when the compass can save time. For instance, large objects in clear water can often be located by a compass search. Therefore, it is a good first step to give a quick look with a compass before setting up the more elaborate method of search lines. On many jobs, the familiar "It won't take you any time to find it; I can show you exactly where it is" can be verified or disproved by a compass swim. If the object of the search is not easily located, more elaborate methods are in order if, of course, the object is worth spending time to search for.

A compass is useful anytime directions are important. During inspection work it is quite often necessary to observe and record the orientation of objects or defects underwater. A compass is indispensable for many types of inspection jobs during the collection of data. Also, it is very easy to lose one's sense of direction in turbid water. Surge on the bottom can quickly disorient a diver. While the diver is recording his findings or taking pictures, he can easily lose track of his position. A compass will save time and can be a crucial safety device under these circumstances.

Where the water is dark or turbid, a compass can be a guide. For work inside a non-magnetic enclosure, a compass may be the only guide in and out. Areas of danger to be avoided such as intake structures or electric cables can be mapped and avoided. At night a compass is instrumental in finding direction and location and may turn out to be the only reliable method of direction-finding a diver has in the dark. For long swims, swims that require precise return routes and for swims through thick growth such as kelp, a compass is irreplaceable.

PRINCIPLE OF COMPASS OPERATION

As early as 121 A.D., the Chinese were aware that an iron rod, brought near natural magnetic rock, would acquire and retain the property of magnetism. If freely suspended about a vertical axis, the rod would then align itself approximately in a north-south direction. The magnetic field of the earth resembles roughly the field of a uniformly magnetized sphere (Fig. 10-1). The principle of operation behind a compass is that a smaller magnet brought into the larger magnetic field of the earth will align itself along a line of force of the larger magnet.

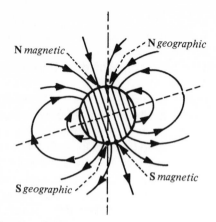

Fig. 10-1. Uniformly magnetized sphere (ideal).

The earth's axis of rotation designates *geographic* or true north and south. *Magnetic* north and south poles are theoretically on a slightly different axis. *Magnetic* north and south always vary from true north and south by a certain amount. The earth's magnetic field, however, is not as symmetrical as Figure 10-1. The magnetic *variation* anywhere on the earth's surface varies irregularly and also changes with time. A compass needle (or a freely suspended bar magnet) will, therefore, align itself along one of the lines of force in the earth's complex magnetic field. The needle will then be establishing a line of *direction* which is generally neither geographic north or south, nor the true direction of the magnetic pole. It is, however, a relatively constant line of direction in any particular place which may be corrected to establish true directions. For navigation over long distances, compass correction to true direction is crucial. For the working diver, the problem of accurate mapping requires establishing true direction. However, some applications of underwater compass work require only relative directions, in which case the diver's concern is reduced to local magnetic attractions and compass *deviation* only. These will be discussed and dealt with in later sections.

THE DIVER'S COMPASS

Two types of wrist compass are generally used for underwater work; the moveable compass card with fixed lubber's line (Fig. 10-2), or the moveable needle with adjustable bezel and fixed lubber's line (Fig. 10-3). The lubber's line is the same on any compass, it is the line along which direction is sighted. The lubber's line reads an angle relative to the north direction indicated by the compass card or the compass needle.

Compass cards and bezels are graduated by *degrees* or by *points* or by a combination of degrees and points. Three hundred sixty degrees indicates 1 complete revolution on a circle. The circle on a compass card or a bezel

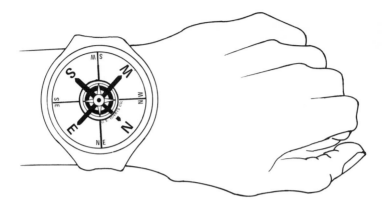

Fig. 10-2. Moveable card compass.

marked by degrees originates at north (being zero) and proceeds clockwise around the card or bezel. The compass traditionally was marked by points, the cardinal points of the compass being the 4 basic directions, north, east, south, and west, east being 90° clockwise from north, south being 180° clockwise from north, and west being 270° clockwise from north. Each cardinal point therefore designated a quadrant or quarter circle on the card. Intercardinal points fell half way between each cardinal point indicating directions northeast (45°), southeast (135°), southwest (225°) and northwest (315°). This process of subdivision continued to 8 points in each quadrant which were further divided to quarter points. The directions indicated by points are seldom used now except for the cardinal and intercardinal points. It is more accurate for the diver to work with directions indicated in degrees where possible. The cheaper models of the wrist compass have a moveable compass card marked by cardinals and intercardinals only and are not recommended for accuracy beyond these basic 8 directions. The most accurate type of wrist compass for underwater work has the moveable needle with adjustable bezel graduated in degrees. Further discussion will be confined to use of the needle and bezel type only.

The bezel on a compass is marked in the same manner as the compass card. While the compass card operates by rotating "with the needle" so to speak, the bezel is operated by the diver, and the needle moves independently of the bezel dial. This affords a more useful instrument to the diver. Whereas the compass card must be read by the lubber's line and course direction numbers must be constantly scrutinized, the bezel can be set on course (indicated by the lubber's line) and the needle is observed so that it does not vary from the marks on the bezel dial.

The course which is chosen is designated by an angle measured clockwise from north. This angle is formed by the lubber's line and the compass needle.

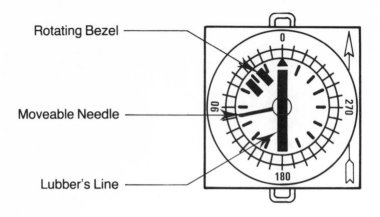

Fig. 10-3. Rotating bezel.

Read in degrees, the angle is called the *azimuth*. It is set by rotating the bezel until the lubber's line indicates the desired reading. The course is followed by aligning the needle between the 2 marks on the bezel. To read a direction, the lubber's line is pointed in the desired direction, the bezel is rotated until the marks fall alongside the needle, and the angle is read on the bezel where the lubber's line points.

Once a return course is taken, a *back azimuth* is computed and set on the compass. If only 1 line of direction was taken, the back azimuth is computed by adding 180° to the original course if the reading was less than 180°, or if the reading was greater than 180°, by subtracting 180° from the original course. With the rotating bezel, this is only a matter of setting the dial opposite to its original course reading.

VARIATION

If we assume the earth is a sphere which rotates about an axis, we designate the axis by true north and true south poles. If we were to pass a plane through the north and south poles (Fig. 10-4), it would form a circle on the earth's surface. Circles which pass through the north and south pole in this manner are called meridians of longitude. If we were to pass a series of planes perpendicular to the polar axis, but not passing through the center of the earth except at the equator, these circles would be called parallels of latitude.

Longitude is measured in degrees from the prime meridian (0°). The prime meridian passes from the north pole through Greenwich, England, to the south pole. Therefore, longitude is measured in degrees east or degrees west of the prime meridian to a maximum of 180° in either direction. Latitude is measured from the equator (0°) either north or south to a maximum of 90° at the poles (Fig. 10-5).

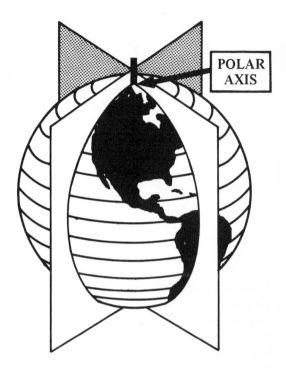

Fig. 10-4. Meridians of longitude.

The intersecting lines formed by latitude and longitude determine true position on the earth. The direction the compass needle indicates would, ideally, be aligned with a meridian of longitude and designated true north anywhere. We already know, however, that this is generally not the case. The compass needle points to magnetic north which lies along the magnetic meridian at that location (assuming there are no deviations or local disturbances which we will discuss later).

The angle between the true meridian and the magnetic meridian is called the *variation*. Variation is dependent upon the earth's magnetic field in a particular location and is *not* the angle between the magnetic poles and the true poles. The compass, therefore, does not necessarily point to either the true pole or the magnetic pole. Variation changes with location and with time. The variation at any particular location is relatively constant with a small annual change. To determine the variation in any location, a *chart rose* is used. Variation is given in degrees east or degrees west. Navigation charts issued by the National Ocean Survey have a chart rose printed on them which indicates the local variation and the annual change (Fig. 10-6). Whenever precise mapping is to be done, a suitable chart of the area should be obtained. Furthermore, it should be a recent chart since annual change cannot be predicted accurately. Change is only a guess based on the trend of prior observations. Sudden changes do occur. Therefore, do not use old charts.

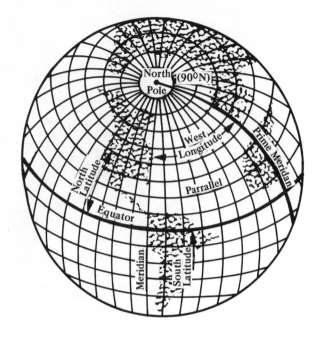

Fig. 10-5. Latitude and longitude.

LOCATIONAL DISTURBANCES

There are some locations where irregular disturbances in the earth's magnetic field will affect the compass. These are rare and occur over relatively small areas. Charts will indicate where these occur. While swimming, however, the diver must be wary of submerged magnetic objects which may affect his compass. A sunken automobile or a wreck, for example, can throw the compass needle off. When working around structures and doing survey work, the diver must be aware of local disturbances from debris. Also, when determining positions or locations on the face of concrete, he must be aware of buried reinforcing rods.

DEVIATION

In addition to the magnetic field of the earth, a diver wearing metallic objects such as scuba tanks or helmets creates a magnetic force of his own which affects his compass. The compass needle then deviates from its alignment with the magnetic meridian. The angle which the needle moves from its proper alignment with the earth's magnetic field is called *deviation*.

Recall that variation changes with location. Compass deviation changes with course *direction*. The reason is that the compass needle is subject to two

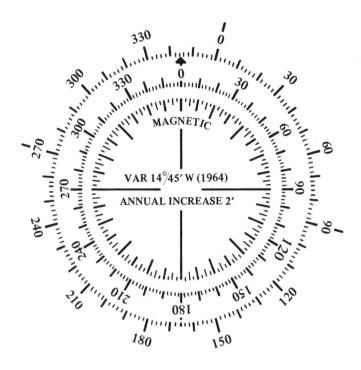

Fig. 10-6. Typical chart rose.

magnetic forces (earth's magnetic field and the diver's equipment). It therefore aligns itself with the resultant of those forces. When the force created by the diver's equipment is aligned with magnetic north, there is zero deviation. When the equipment force is perpendicular to magnetic north, there is maximum deviation. The diver who requires accuracy for his work will need to tabulate a deviation chart for the equipment he is wearing. If he is swimming with a buddy in scuba, the buddy's equipment must be accounted for as well. During the work the buddy must be near and remain in the same position relative to the compass.

A chart is prepared by taking readings at the surface with no equipment. Directions are marked according to readings (depending on the work, this will be as many directions as required). Equipment is then donned and directions are taken again. Observation is made of the difference between readings with no equipment and readings with full equipment. The differences are then tabulated as deviaton in degrees E or degrees W. If a commercial or previously prepared chart is available, the chart rose is aligned with the compass to magnetic north with no equipment nearby. Equipment is then donned and readings are taken, using the chart rose to determine deviation.

CORRECTING THE COMPASS

A course direction can be indicated by any 1 of 3 different names; the compass course, the magnetic course, or the true course. Despite the fact that the 3 readings may differ numerically, they all indicate the same direction. If the compass is corrected for deviation, it gives the magnetic reading. If the compass is corrected for deviation and variation, it gives the true reading. The algebraic sum of variation and deviation is called *compass error*.

While using the compass underwater, the diver observes and records his bearings by compass readings. When readings are mapped, they are customarily corrected to true directions. Maps and charts are prepared according to true directions with magnetic directions indicated as well. It becomes necessary at times to be able to convert directions into any of the 3 ways of indicating direction.

Example 10-1:

You obtain a recent mariner's chart for a location you are to work in. The chart indicates for your location that the variation is 10°W. From a dock on-shore, it is known that a wooden wreck lies 100 yards due east (true direction). You have already drawn up a deviation chart for the job on which you have found:

Full gear compass reading	Magnetic reading from chart rose	Deviation
80°	70°	10° W
86°	80°	6° W
92°	90°	2° W
98°	100°	2° E
105°	110°	5° E

What must be your compass course to find the wreck?

Answer:

The true direction due east is 90°

$$\text{Magnetic direction} = \text{true direction} \pm \begin{matrix} \text{west variation} \\ \text{or} \\ \text{east variation} \end{matrix}$$

$$= 90° + 10°W = 100°$$

$$\text{Compass direction} = \text{magnetic direction} + \text{west deviation} \\ - \text{east deviation}$$

$$= 100° - 2° E^* = 98°$$

*Remember deviation is the angle formed with the *magnetic* meridian.

Example 10-2:
When you find the wreck you observe, by your compass, that she lies at an angle of 90° from bow to stern, what is the *true* angle?

Answer:
When you come ashore, you set your compass at 90°, remove your gear and find the deviation. Then, either add or subtract the deviation (depending upon which direction the deviation is) from 90°. You then have the magnetic course reading. From that you subtract 10° (the westerly variation) to get the true angle.

SUMMARY OF RELATIONS

Azimuth is the compass reading formed by the angle between the lubber's line and the needle—read in degrees.

Back Azimuth is the compass reading to follow in order to return, computed by adding 180° if azimuth was less than 180°, subtracting 180° if azimuth was more than 180°.

Variation is the angle between the magnetic meridian and the true meridian.

Chart Rose designates variation at location and annual change.

Deviation is the angle between compass needle and magnetic meridian caused by diver's equipment.

To correct compass reading to true reading:
Add easterly variation, deviation
Subtract westerly variation, deviation

To convert true reading to compas reading:
Add westerly variation, deviation
Subtract easterly variation, deviation

CHAPTER 11: WAVES & CURRENTS VS. THE WORKING DIVER

The diver working underwater is confronted by powerful hydrodynamic forces. The motion of water is caused by disturbances which upset the balance of the fluid. In turn, the water restores its equilibrium by internal fluid motion. Disturbing forces influencing the motion of water cause waves at the surface and currents within the fluid.

Waves and currents exert forces on the working diver and his equipment which must be understood and dealt with accordingly. Waves are generated by wind, tide, air pressure and earthquakes. Currents are generated by wind, tide, gravity and the earth's rotation. Of basic concern to the working diver are wind waves and all currents.

WIND WAVES

When the wind blows over the surface of the water, it transmits mechanical energy directly to the water distorting the air-sea interface. These distortions are waves on the water surface which build in height and length as they gain energy from the wind. Waves are a phenomenon unto themselves for they move through the water very rapidly without transporting much of the water along the way. This is verified by observing a floating object in the path of a wave. As the wave crest approaches, the object will move forward in the water, pause as the trough approaches, then move backward in the trough almost to where it began. The motion the object makes is almost circular with a slight advance in the direction the wave is traveling. The time it takes for the floating object to complete one cycle of motion is called the *wave period*. The wave height is measured from the trough to the crest. Wave length is measured from crest to crest and the frequency of a wave is the inverse of wave period, or the number of crests per second that pass.

As the wind blows, waves will grow in length and height until they reach a limit of height. If there is more wind energy available at that point waves will become longer and longer. How high the waves become will depend upon the force or speed of the wind, how long the wind blows, and the distance over which it blows (fetch). The wind needs force, duration and fetch to build waves.

If the wind blows long enough to reach an energy balance with the sea, the waves will become completely developed. This condition is known as a *fully aroused sea*. If the wind changes direction or diminishes before it has had enough time to reach this energy balance, the waves will not build to their full potential under that wind force. During the time the waves are being driven by the wind, they are called a *sea*. When the influence of the wind that raised them is gone, the waves are referred to as *swell*. Swells have greater wave lengths than do seas and they tend to become smoother and longer in form once the wind is no longer driving them.

Wave steepness is the ratio of wave height to wave length and is one important factor during surface operations. A long smooth swell six feet high is sometimes easier to work with than a "choppy" sea only two feet high. Waves are steeper or choppier during the early part of a blow than when the sea becomes more fully developed.

Currents which run into wavetrains will alter wave length and wave height. This will affect wave steepness. Currents running against the waves will bunch the waves closer together causing the waves to become steeper. If the current runs with the waves, it will spread them farther apart causing the waves to decrease in steepness. During tide rips, this can become very important to the diver. Tide change can bring about sudden alterations of sea surface conditions. Waves appearing safe when the tide is running with the wind can become very choppy and unmanagable in a matter of minutes when the tide changes. Once the waves escape the influence of a current, however, they revert back to their original shape.

Waves which run into each other from different directions or the same direction will temporarily add to or subtract from each other. After combining, they will then pass through each other and continue on unaltered. This can cause confused seas where wavetrains from storms in different locations cross each other.

If not dissipated by shifting winds, waves eventually reach land. As they approach land from deep water, they are influenced as the bottom shoals up under them. Waves in deep water create orbital motions of water particles beneath them (Fig. 11-1). This disturbance diminishes with depth to almost zero at a depth of half the wave length. When the bottom is shallower than half the wavelength, the water particle motion created by the wave begins to interact with the bottom of the sea. Since the bottom cannot be moved up and down, the particle motion of the water at the bottom is restricted to a back and forth movement. This cyclic back and forth movement is called *surge*. As the wave moves into shallower and shallower water, the motion of the water beneath it interacts more and more with the bottom creating stronger and stronger surge. At a point where the depth of the water beneath the wave is 1/20 of the wave length, the particle motion at the top of the wave extends virtually unaltered to the bottom except that orbital motion flattens to a side to side motion at the bottom (Fig. 11-1).

As the wave begins to "feel" the bottom in shallow water, its speed is decreased by the interaction of water motion against the bottom. When waves approach the beach at an oblique angle, the first part of the wave to touch bottom is slowed down allowing the rest of the wave to catch up. There is also a net transport of water along the shoreline because of the interaction. The term *longshore currents* is used to denote currents caused by the waves approaching the beach at an oblique angle. Because the bottom slows the forward part

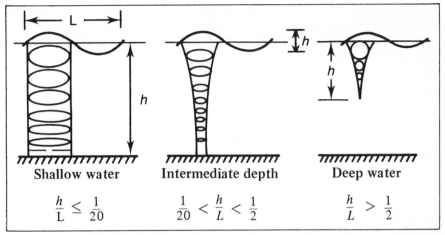

Fig. 11-1. Particle motions beneath waves in the ocean.

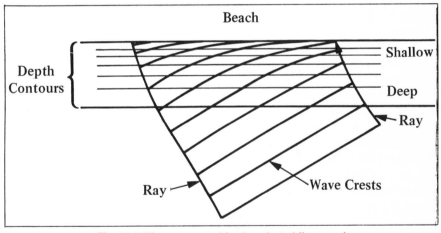

Fig. 11-2. Waves approaching beach at oblique angle.

of a wave allowing the rest of the wave to catch up, waves approach the beach more or less parallel to the shoreline and it is not possible to tell which direction the waves are running offshore from the angle they approach the beach (Fig. 11-2).

Bottom contours in shallow water will have a marked influence on waves either by focusing or defocusing them (Figs. 11-3 and 11-4). As a wave passes over a hill in shallow water, it will cause the part of the wave passing over the hill to slow down. Waves behind will then bunch up. The hill will push the wave height up and perhaps cause the wave form to become unstable and break. The rest of the wave alongside which is not passing over the hill will not be slowed and will run ahead of the wave segment passing over the hill.

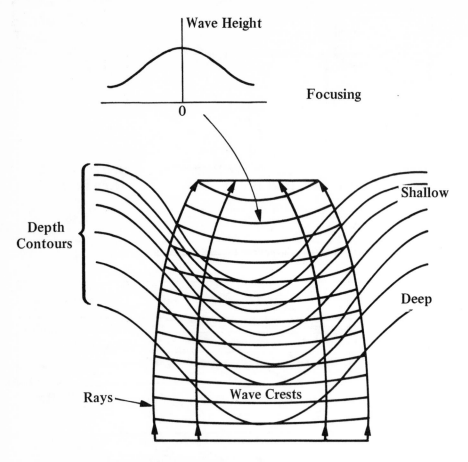

Fig. 11-3. Waves passing over a hill.

Waves passing over a valley in shallow water will speed up due to the reduction of bottom friction. Wavelength will increase causing waves to spread out. The portion of the wave passing over a valley will run ahead of the rest of the wave.

As the wave finally runs ashore, it breaks in *surf* dissipating its energy on the beach. Waves running into shallow water are slowed down by bottom friction. The bottom also pushes up the wave heights resulting in the waves becoming bunched and steeper very quickly. A point of instability is soon reached and the waves topple or break. Depending upon the wave form, wind direction, and bottom contours, breakers will generally be *plunging*, *spilling* or *intermittent* (Fig. 11-5). A plunging breaker goes to pieces in a few seconds leaving almost no remanent of the wave form. A spilling breaker on the other hand slowly unravels its form as it approaches the beach. A wave which is not completely dissipated on the first break may regroup and break again several times before

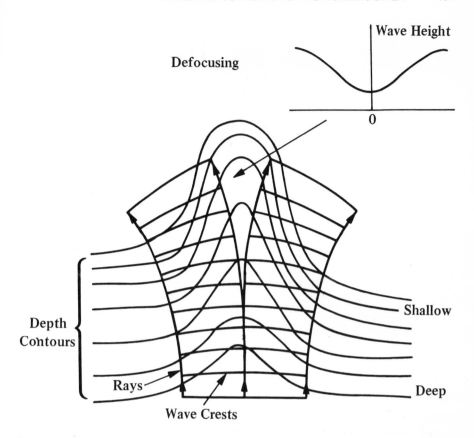

Fig. 11-4. Waves passing over a valley.

the wave form is entirely destroyed. The intermittent breaker is common where the bottom is not evenly sloped toward the beach.

Unlike waves at sea, waves in the surf zone transport water with the wave form. This means any object in the water will be moved with it. For this reason, it becomes important to understand surf power. The potential energy a wave possesses is transformed in the surf zone into real expended energy by water set in motion pounding the solid ground. The water is set in violent motion in the surf zone and possesses great destructive power for this reason. Divers working in the surf zone must be aware of methods to negotiate these powerful forces. Table 11-1 indicates the power of surf.

Waves do not always end up breaking on a sloping beach: they occasionally run against solid vertical walls particularly where manmade bulkheads are present. The wall will not dissipate wave energy if it is immovable. The resulting effect of waves running against immovable vertical walls is wave reflection. Reflected waves will simply change direction and travel on unaltered. Where a wavetrain approaches a vertical wall head on, the reflected

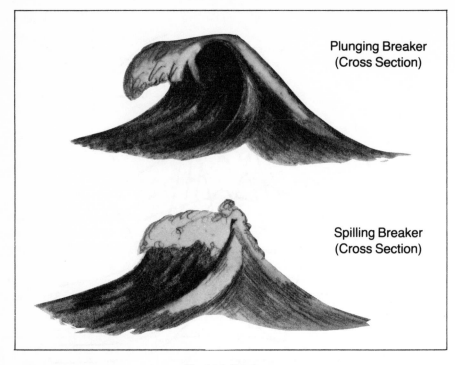

Fig. 11-5. Breakers.

waves will travel directly opposite the oncoming waves and create a *standing wave pattern*. The crest and trough of a standing wave remain in one spot which is called an *antinode* (Fig. 11-6). The motion of standing waves is similar to a vibrating string. The crests of the waves do not travel in a horizontal direction like normal ocean waves, but simply move up and down in one place (the antinode). Since there is no vertical motion at all at the *node*, the water surface is undisturbed.

The water particle motion beneath a standing wave is quite different from the orbital motions beneath a normal traveling wave at sea (Fig. 11-7). At the antinodes of a standing wave the water motion is straight up and down. At the nodes it is side to side. Between the nodes and antinodes, the water particle motion is at an angle inclined toward the antinode. Where standing waves of sufficient size and frequency are present, the diver in the water will be confronted with several difficulties because of water motion around him. If he is close enough to the wall, he may be thrown against the wall *repeatedly*. One of the dangers of being caught in standing waves is the difficulty in moving through them. The nature of the water particle motion will tend to force the diver either to a node where he will be trapped in a cyclic horizontal motion or to an antinode where he will be trapped in a cyclic vertical motion. Standing

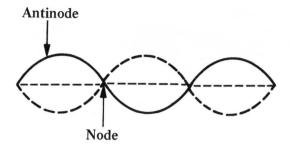

Fig. 11-6. Standing wave pattern.

waves of sufficient size and frequency are therefore difficult to swim through especially at the suface. Care should be taken around structures such as bulkheads, bridges and platforms or around large ships and barges where standing wave patterns might occur.

Table 11-1
Power of Surf

Wave Height trough to crest (ft)	Approximate horsepower per linear foot of wave (water depth = 4 ft)	Approximate horsepower per linear foot of wave (water depth = 10 ft)
2	.66	1
3	1.5	2
4	3	4
5	4	7
6	6	10
7	8	13
8	11	17
9	13	21
10	17	26
11	20	32
12	24	38

Based on the equation; $p = 1/8 \, \rho g H^2 C_g$

where
p = power of surf
ρ = density of water
g = gravity
H = waveheight
C_g = group velocity

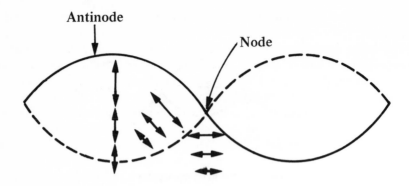

Fig. 11-7. Particle motion beneath a standing wave.

WAVE FORECASTING

There are in existence elaborate methods for predicting the wave heights and frequency according to wind speed, wind duration, fetch and water depth. These will not be dealt with in this book. Table 11-2, however, is included as a guide for estimating conditions of wind and sea.

PRESSURE FLUCTUATION BENEATH A WAVE

A diver at a 10 foot decompression stop may encounter some danger from the pressure fluctuation beneath a large amplitude wave under the right circumstances. A diver working on any fixed structure in shallow water beneath a heavy sea may be subject to possible embolism due to the magnitude of pressure fluctuation above him. There is at least 1 recorded diving accident which suggests that embolism occurred due to a large wave passing over a diver fixed to a pipe (1975 National Oceanographic Atmospheric Administration Helgaland Project).

The pressure beneath a wave depends upon many variables. Of concern to the diver, however, is the possibility of pressure *fluctuation* of sufficient magnitude to present the danger of air embolism or decompression problems. Fortunately, the fluctuation of pressure beneath a wave is damped out with depth. Also, the magnitude of waves that might produce any decompression problems preclude any sane diving operations. Further, the diver would have to be fixed relative to the waves before he would experience any pressure fluctuation, otherwise he simply is lifted and dropped with the passing wave form. The problem is, therefore, reduced to evaluating when an *air embolism* might possibly occur due to the pressure fluctuation.

It is conceivable that a diver fixed to a piling or any structure at a 10 foot decompression stop could be inhaling just as the crest of a wave passes and not begin exhalation before the trough passes. He would then experience a rapid pressure drop around the lungs resulting in over distention and air embolism.

The wave would have to be of sufficient amplitude in order to create an overpressure of around 4.4 fsw. It would also have to be in a frequency range which corresponds roughly with the diver's breathing cycle (assuming, of course, the diver was not holding his breath, in which case, any wave of sufficient amplitude could cause embolism). Finally, there would have to be water of sufficient depth below the diver for waves meeting these criteria even to occur. Figure 11-8 represents the conditions of pressure fluctuation caused by waves over a diver fixed at a 10 foot decompression stop with at least 50 feet of water depth below him. The analysis done was based on an overpressure of 4.4 fsw being a danger and the equation:

$$P_n = (P_a + \rho gh) + \rho g \eta \frac{\cosh 2\pi \frac{(d-h)}{L}}{\cosh 2\pi \frac{d}{L}} \qquad [11.1]$$

where

P_n = pressure beneath a wave at depth = h

P_a = atmospheric pressure

ρ = density of water

g = gravity

h = depth beneath surface

η = wave amplitude

d = bottom depth of water

L = wave length

CURRENTS

Currents are one of the most difficult problems a working diver must contend with. Any time water is moving in one direction at a given speed, the force exerted on the diver is proportional to the water velocity squared. In other words, if the current speed doubles, the force against the diver increases four times.

Currents are caused by tides, and by wind in some instances. Currents are also caused by waves (longshore and rip currents, for example) and in rivers by gravity. Ocean circulation currents occur for a variety of reasons all of which are not understood.

River currents will be most rapid where the depth shoals or the river narrows. The reason for this is that the same volume must pass through a smaller area resulting in more rapid flow.

Currents caused by tide will run most rapidly at the surface and may become somewhat slower at the bottom depending upon contours and roughness of the bottom. Currents caused by the wind occur mostly at the surface.

Table 11-2 Wind Spee

Beau-fort number	Wind Speed				Nautical	U. S. Weather Bureau Term	Hydrographic Office	
	knots	mph	meters per second	km per hour			Term and height of waves, in ft.	Code
0	under 1	under 1	0.0- 0.2	under 1	Calm	Light	Calm, 0	0
1	1-3	1-3	0.3- 1.5	1-5	Light air		Smooth, less than 1	1
2	4-6	4-7	1.6- 3.3	6-11	Light Breeze		Slight, 1-3	2
3	7-10	8-12	3.4- 5.4	12-19	Gentle Breeze	Gentle	Moderate, 3-5	3
4	11-16	13-18	5.5- 7.9	20-28	Moderate Breeze	Moderate		
5	17-21	19-24	8.0-10.7	29-38	Fresh Breeze	Fresh	Rough, 5-8	4
6	22-27	25-31	10.8-13.8	39-49	Strong Breeze			
7	28-33	32-38	13.9-17.1	50-61	Moderate Gale	Strong		
8	34-40	39-46	17.2-20.7	62-74	Fresh Gale	Gale	Very rough, 8-12	5
9	41-47	47-54	20.8-24.4	75-88	Strong Gale		High, 12-20	6
10	48-55	55-63	24.5-28.4	89-102	Whole Gale		Very high, 20-40	7
11	56-63	64-72	28.5-32.6	103-117	Storm		Mountainous, 40 and higher	8
12	64-71	73-82	32.7-36.9	118-133	Hurri-cane	Hurri-cane	Confused	9
13	72-80	83-92	37.0-41.4	134-149				
14	81-89	93-103	41.5-46.1	150-166				
15	90-99	104-114	46.2-50.9	167-183				
16	100-108	115-125	51.0-56.0	184-201				
17	109-118	126-136	56.1-61.2	202-220				

(Source: U.S. Navy Hydrographic Office)

International		Estimating wind speed	
Term and height of waves, in ft.	Code	Effects observed at sea	Effects observed on land
Calm, glassy	0	Sea like mirror.	Calm; smoke rises vertically.
		Ripples with appearance of scales; no foam crests.	Smoke, drift indicates wind direction; vanes do not move.
Rippled, 0-1	1	Small wavelets; crests of glassy appearance, not breaking.	Wind felt on face, leaves rustle; vanes begin to move.
Smooth, 1-2	2	Large wavelets; crests begin to break, scattered whitecaps.	Leaves, small twigs in constant motion; light flags extended.
Slight, 2-4	3	Small waves, becoming longer; numerous whitecaps.	Dust, leaves, and loose paper raised up, small branches move.
Moderate, 4-8		Moderate waves, taking longer form, many whitecaps; some spray.	Small trees in leaf begin to sway.
Rough, 8-13	5	Larger waves forming; whitecaps everywhere; more spray.	Larger branches of trees in motion; whistling heard in wires.
Very rough, 13-20	6	Sea heaps up; white foam from breaking waves begin to be blown in streaks.	Whole trees in motion; resistance felt in walking against wind.
		Moderately high waves of greater length; edges of crests begin to break into sprindrift; foam is blown in well-marked streaks.	Twigs and small branches broken off trees; progress generally impeded.
		High waves; sea begins to roll; dense streaks of foam; spray may reduce visibility.	Slight structural damage occurs; slate blown from roofs.
High, 20-30	7	Very high waves with overhanging crests; sea takes white appearance as foam is blown in very dense streaks; rolling is heavy and visibility reduced.	Seldom experienced on land; trees broken or uprooted; considerable structural damage occurs.
Very high, 30-45	8	Exceptionally high waves; sea covered with white foam patches; visibility still more reduced.	Very rarely experienced on land; usually accompanied by widespread damage.
Phenomenal, over 45	9	Air filled with foam; sea completely white with driving spray; visibility greatly reduced.	

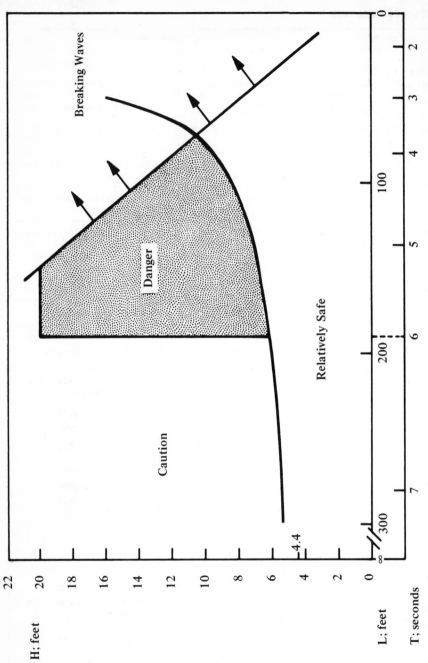

Fig. 11-8. Waves which may cause embolism at a 10 ft decompression stop (depth of 50 ft or greater below diver) based on airy wave equations and overpressure of 4.4 FSW.

(Source: U.N. Schenck)

Table 11-3 Approximate Current Drag Force on Submerged Diver

Current Speed (knots)	Force on Diver Standing Facing current (lbs) (maximum profile)	Force on Diver Horizontal Facing current (lbs) (Minimum profile)
1/2	6	1
1	23	4
1 1/2	52	9
2	92	15
2 1/2	144	24
3	207	36
3 1/2	282	47
4	369	61
4 1/2	467	78
5	576	96

The drag force a current will exert on a diver can be found by evaluating

$$F_D = 1/2\,\rho V^2 C_D A$$

where

F_D = drag force on any object

P   = density of fluid

V   = velocity of fluid

C_D = coefficient of Drag

A   = area exposed to current

Values for C_D are determined experimentally. The area profile a diver presents to the current will depend on whether he is standing, sitting or lying horizontally, also what type of equipment he is wearing and, finally, whether he is facing the current or is sideways to it. How much current a diver can work in will depend on his physical strength, how much lead weight he puts on, and what kind of equipment he is wearing. Table 11-3 represents some general values of current force on a diver in two different positions.

At Dolby Dam, Lake Millinocket, Maine, a diver assists in placing forms 65 feet deep and 55 feet underneath the dam to weight it and strengthen the entire structure so that trash screens can be dewatered. The dam was moving downstream at a rate of 2 inches a year and lifting 1 inch. To stop this action, 2000 yards of concrete were pumped into the forms. The diver wears a Kirby-Morgan band mask and holds his lifeline and air hose. Hanging from his belt is an underwater light needed to work while penetrating 55 feet into the dam.

CHAPTER 12: UNDERWATER LIGHT AND SOUND

Clear vision underwater is not a typical condition for the working diver. Several factors exist which alter light optically as it passes through the air-water interface and travels into the depths where the diver works. Even if the diver brings his own light source, he is not assured of any degree of visibility when the water is very turbid.

Sound underwater also has distinctly different characteristics from sound in air. With the human ear, it is difficult underwater to distinguish direction and the distance of a sound source. Bubble noise from the diver's air supply further complicates hearing ability because of the level of "background noise" bubbles create.

With the reduction of sight and hearing capabilities, the working diver often performs tasks not unlike a blind-deaf man might who is further handicapped by an inability to smell or taste anything but salt and whose fingers and hands are perpetually numbed by the water and gloves he wears. Despite these handicaps understanding the behavior of light and sound underwater will enhance the diver's perception and increase his ability to work effectively. If the expense justifies it, technology offers assistance, and there are available alternatives to "working blind" which are worth examining.

PENETRATION OF VISIBLE LIGHT

When sunlight strikes the surface of the ocean, it is partly reflected and partly transmitted into the water. The amount of reflected sunlight reduces the extent of light available to penetrate the depth of water. How much light is reflected at the surface depends upon the angle of the sun (time of day) and how rough the surface of the sea is. Waves will change the angle at which the sun strikes the surface at any given point and may cause light to be reflected or transmitted with greater intensity depending upon wave shape and where light strikes the wave form. Since they introduce a fairly uniform set of angles through which light is transmitted, smooth rounded waves tend to focus direct light. The focusing effect occurs because the wave form creates a crude lens. Beneath the wave, narrow bands of focused light travel across the bottom in shallow water.

Wave shape will sometimes be more steep and pointed at the top rather than round and smooth like a lens. When the wave shape becomes steeper and pointed (trochoidal), it tends to resemble a crude prism which will break light down into "rainbows" in shallow water.

When the sea is aroused enough to create white caps, areas of foam will screen light from passing through the surface causing significant loss of light

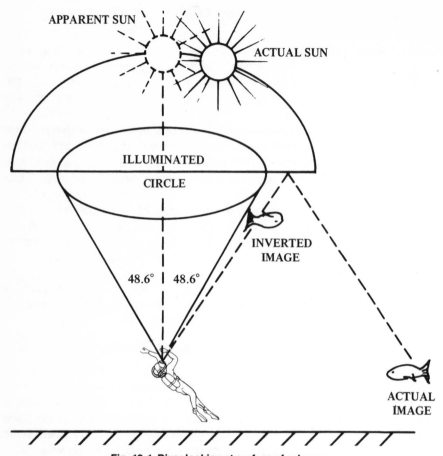

Fig. 12-1. Diver looking at surface of calm sea.

beneath them. Seaweed and other objects at the surface will also serve to block light below. Waves of sufficient size disturb the bottom and stir up sediment which further reduces visibility.

REFRACTION

Once light has passed the interface of air and water, it is immediately bent (refracted) due to the change in density between air and water (Snell's law). The bending of light causes the apparent position of an object viewed across the interface to differ from its actual position. The sun viewed from underwater therefore, appears to be higher in the sky than it actually is, and the horizon appears at an angle of 48.6 degrees from the vertical. Owing to this effect, the diver looking up at the surface of a calm sea will observe an illuminated circle overhead. In shallow water, the sun may appear as a bright spot in the circle; but at greater depths, the effect is diffused so that a diver will only observe a

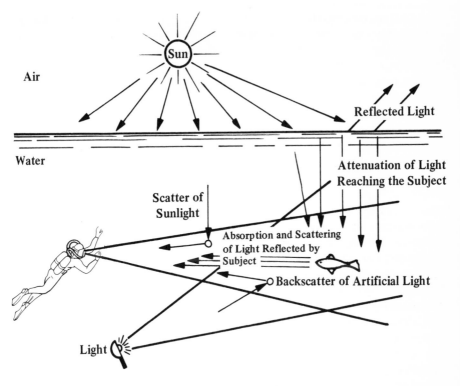

Fig. 12-2. Effect of light underwater.

bright illuminated circle overhead (Fig. 12-1). Beyond the edge of the circle, the surface behaves as a mirror reflecting light emitted from the bottom which produces an inverted image of any object in the surrounding water.

SCATTERING AND ABSORPTION

Light rays in the water are subject to *scattering* and *absorption* (Fig. 12-2). Scattering is due to collision of light rays with reflective particles; absorption is due to an energy transformation from light to (mostly) heat. The transformation takes place between light rays and water molecules and between light rays and absorptive particles.

Particles suspended in the water will generally partially absorb light and partially scatter light. Some particles, however, will almost completely absorb light, others will almost completely scatter light. Scattered light will bounce off in many uneven directions, then collide with other particles or add to other light rays going in the same direction. Eventually, scattered light will either add to the direct light or brighten the background (backscatter). Backscatter reduces the contrast between objects of vision and the background. As we shall see, backscatter problems are more severe for portable illumination systems co-located with the diver.

Scattering can also be caused by abrupt changes in water density (change of refractive index). Heavy rains produce water layers of different temperature and salinity. When such layers are disturbed and partially mixed, optical distortion and scattering occur. Thermal pollution and other contaminants from outfalls may cause similar effects upon mixing with surrounding water.

Absorption of light passing through water occurs on a "selective basis." White light is a mixture of many different colors of light and contains the entire spectrum of visible and invisible light. On one end of the spectrum is the ultraviolet light which occurs at the highest frequency (it has the shortest wavelength). The spectrum then passes through the visible range of violet-blue-green-yellow-orange and red to the infra-red range which has the longest wavelength. As the light mixture passes through water, water molecules and their components are affected by certain wavelengths of light. High frequency light waves (ultraviolet) cause vibration of tiny sub-atomic particles called electrons. Low frequency light waves (infra-red) cause vibration of entire water molecules (large by comparison). The energy of light waves which excites atomic and molecular particles is then absorbed by those particles and transformed into another form of energy which results mainly in heating the water. The maximum absorption effect thus occurs at each end of the light spectrum and spills over from each end into the visible spectrum. Therefore, red light is absorbed selectively first at one end and violet disappears from the other. In the visible spectrum light is more broadly absorbed from the red end of the spectrum eliminating orange and yellow. The result is that in pure distilled water and in clear oceanic water, blue-green light is *transmitted* better than any other wavelength of light and accounts for the predominance of blue-green light under clear water.

Suspended particles and dissolved matter of a certain color wil absorb light more strongly from the shorter wavelengths (blues) and sometimes cause a shift in the color of light transmitted in the water. The color shift may cause the water to appear green (common near the coast), yellow, brown, or even red depending on the substance and its concentration.

For this reason, river water often appears yellow or brown because silt suspended in the water selectively absorbs enough blue and green light to shift the color toward yellow-brown.

USE OF ARTIFICIAL LIGHT

Supplemental lighting is often required to achieve adequate light levels for vision, photography, or TV surveys underwater. The working diver is frequently called upon to illuminate his work area either to perform his task or to record what he observes. Where color balance or good image contrast are necessary for photography, in-water lights are indispensable. Techniques for underwater photography are beyond the scope of this book; but it is useful for the working diver to have some familiarity with the lighting techniques used in underwater photography as a tool for effectively illuminating his work areas.

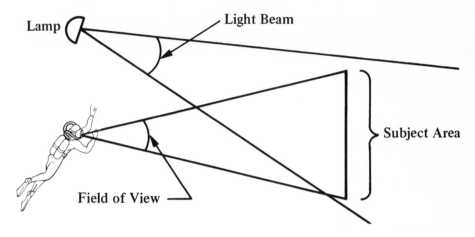

Fig. 12-3. Lighting geometry.

When the diver carries a light sources with him underwater, the distance the light must travel in order to accomplish illumination of an object is minimized. As a result, the light will suffer less attenuation as it travels the relatively shorter path from source to subject to diver than it would if it had to travel all the way from the surface. A light source of high intensity is especially important when it is necessary to determine the true color of an object at depth.

If the water were always free from suspended particles, illumination would be a simple matter of carrying a light source powerful enough to do the job. Since water is seldom free of such particles, the diver must deal with *backscatter*, one of the most difficult problems hampering effective illumination of underwater work. Backscatter occurs when light from a source is reflected in the direction of the diver from suspended particles in the water.

When light strikes suspended particles in the water, it illuminates the particles along with the surrounding water creating background effect (glare). Glare reduces the contrast between the object of vision and its surroundings. Unfortunately, increasing the illumination intensity to achieve better image lighting also increases the glare and may elevate the glare enough to wash out the image altogether.

The simplest method of reducing glare caused by backscatter is by careful placement of the light source. When the light source and the observer are in the same location, suspended particles in front of the observer's eyes will be directly illuminated and obscure the field of vision. Thus glare is at its most severe level when the diver is closest to the light source. This kind of backscatter may be eliminated by moving the light source off to one side (Fig. 12-3). As a practical matter, a diver carrying a hand-held light is somewhat limited in his ability to arrange lighting geometry, but the technique of moving the light to one side will definitely improve his vision. Underwater flash pictures are also improved by this technique. When conditions require more adequate lighting,

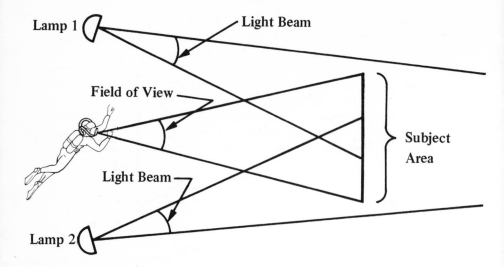

Fig. 12-3. Multiple lighting geometry.

two or more lights staged as shown (Fig. 12-4) will minimize the loss of contrast due to backscatter. To minimize all aspects of backscatter, the observer should position himself as close to the center line as possible.

Lighting geometry is not the only technique available to reduce backscattering effects. By using a light source with a peak spectral response in the blue-green region, contrast and image illumination can be improved. Since light traveling from the source to the target and back to the observer will be color filtered by the relatively long water path, it will have its strongest energy in the blue-green region (due to absorption of other colors). The close-in backscatter, however, will not lose its energy in the rest of the color spectrum due to the relatively shorter path through which it travels. If, however, the light were mainly blue-green to begin with, the ratio of backscatter intensity (glare) to the object of vision would be reduced because the light source, being blue-green, effectively filters out some of the close-in backscatter response. The same effect is achieved by using an orange-red filter on a camera.

The glare from backscatter can be reduced by filtering its response on the red end of the spectrum. Contrast is thereby improved by adjusting the foreground light (blue-green) to complement the distant image rather than the close-in backscatter (red).

UNDERWATER SOUND

Communication capability greatly improves diver safety and efficiency. Predictably, however, numerous difficulties are encountered when reliable voice communication must be established underwater. In order to comprehend the factors tending to disrupt and alter sound underwater, a few basic principles of sound behavior and speech must be understood. Underwater acoustics is a much studied phenomenon with interest to all disciplines of undersea work and research. This section, however, will limit its scope to the concern of the working diver.

Sound behavior is similar to light behavior in that sound and light are wave phenomena. Sound waves, however, are waves of pressure rather than radiation. Vibrating objects produce sound which propagates in a wave pattern of moving molecules through the transmitting medium (air, water, etc.). Since sound pressure is transmitted by molecules, the more closely packed, or denser the medium of molecular matter, the more efficiently the sound waves are transmitted. Sound is received or detected by vibration response to the sound in an eardrum or microphone diaphragm (called sympathetic vibration).

Water is an excellent conductor of sound because the molecular structure of water is dense relative to air. The speed of sound under water is about 5,000 feet per second compared to around 1,100 feet per second in air. Sound in the water therefore travels more efficiently than in air, about 4 times as fast. What, then, are the difficulties for the diver?

Directional discrimination by the human ear is dependent upon the ability to detect the difference in time of arrival of sound in each ear. Since sound travels so fast underwater, the time interval between arrival at each ear is indiscernible. It is therefore difficult to determine the direction of any sound source underwater. Another negative characteristic of sound travel underwater from the diver's point of view is the apparent failure to lose intensity over distances which are significant to the diver. For example, so far as the diver is concerned, a power boat could be nearly overhead or 100 feet away and coming from any direction.

Voice communication underwater is adversely affected for many reasons, not the least of which is the fact that sound originating in air will not transmit much into water and sound originating in water will not transmit much into air. Due to the large difference in densities, a sound wave will be mostly reflected at the interface of air and water. The problem which arises with voice transmission through water is that vocal chords and eardrums were meant to transmit and receive vibrations in air. Talking underwater is, therefore, virtually impossible from diver to diver unless electronic communications are used, or the water between them can be eliminated (helmet to helmet contact). Other communication problems are encountered because of equipment, pressure and gas mixtures.

Equipment worn by the diver for breathing purposes underwater creates noise during operation, restricts the diver's vocal mechanisms, and alters the quality of diver voice sound by reverberation within the mask or helmet. Noise from equipment occurs several ways. Air intake jets in the mask or helmet create noise from the air expanding and rushing into the helmet or mask. Intake and exhaust valves set in vibration from gas flow sometimes chatter.

Finally, exhaust bubbles escaping into the water create noise. The effect of the noise is two-fold; first it introduces a level of background noise which interferes with the diver's voice transmission and his ear reception. Second, it interfers with the diver's ability to hear himself speak. By not hearing his own speech, the diver's automatic self-regulating voice control mechanisms are inhibited and he may tend to shout and distort his speech.

Mouthpieces, face masks, and helmets will also tend to restrict the free movement of various voice mechanisms. A mouthpiece reduces the use of tongue and lips for articulation of speech. A full face mask often presses the chin into the throat making it difficult to move the jaw properly and placing pressure on the vocal chords. Some helmets use a neck ring assembly which puts perssure on the throat area affecting the vocal chords. Demand air system valves are designed to maintain gas pressure inside the mask or helmet slightly higher than ambient water pressure to ensure that water does not enter the mask or helmet. This requires the diver to speak against the slightly elevated back pressure causing some speech distortion.

The airspace within the mask or helmet creates an acoustic chamber where sound from the diver's voice will reverberate. A helmet offers greater air space and produces the better quality sound. Also, the diver's ears are dry and directly exposed to the sound of his own voice allowing better feedback to his auditory self-regulating mechanisms. A mask provides less air space for sound to reverberate and the distortion is usually greater. In a mask, the diver does not directly hear the sound of his own voice; this probably causes him to shout a little more.

Pressure and gas mixtures associated with deep diving operations strongly affect the quality of the diver's speech. The effect of pressure with depth produces a steady decline in speech intelligibility. Voice level rises and the tone takes on a nasal quality. The reasons for this are not yet completely understood, but may be partially due to elevated back pressures in the apparatus which alter the vocal chords' response frequency. When gas mixtures are employed to reduce the narcotic effect of nitrogen in deep dives, they tend to change the vocal sounds a diver makes because of the increased speed of sound in the gas mixture. Helium-oxygen is the primary mix used, and helium adversely affects speech in proportion to its percentage in the breathing mixture. A 90% helium content generally renders speech almost completely unintelligible.

Beyond the problem of direction, distance and voice communication, underwater sound of given intensity will be heard more clearly and rapidly than the same noise level at a given distance in air. Physical pain or damage can therefore occur from operations producing dangerous noise levels underwater which would ordinarily be safe if conducted in air.

The sound level of some high powered air tools approaches the pain threshold. Most damaging is the shock effect caused by the pressure wave of underwater explosions.

CONCLUSION

Diving calculations require careful consideration of all known variables before numbers are used. When making calculations, a principle ground rule should always be kept in mind: Allow a margin of safety. The formulas presented in this book will provide safe calculations. However, where new conditions for diving (as illustrated by high altitude diving) occur, do not make assumptions before the effects of the new conditions are understood.

Finally, it goes without saying, safety should take precedence over economy. (Some are willing to risk safety for reasons of economy.) Although nothing is absolutely safe, compromising generally accepted margins of safety is asking for trouble.

Enjoy what you do, do it safely, and make a profit.

USEFUL MATH

V = volume
A = area
C = circumference
π = 3.1416

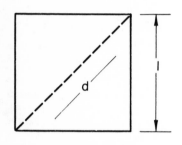

SQUARE

$A = l^2$
$d = l\sqrt{2}$

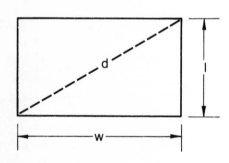

RECTANGLE

$A = lw$
$d = \sqrt{(l^2 + W^2)}$

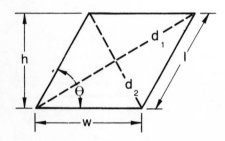

PARALLELOGRAM

$A = wh = wl \sin \Theta$
$d_1 = \sqrt{[(w + h \cot \Theta)^2 + h^2]}$
$d_2 = \sqrt{[(w - h \cot \Theta)^2 + h^2]}$

170

TRAPEZOID

$$A = \frac{a+b}{2}h = mh$$

$$m = \frac{a+b}{2}$$

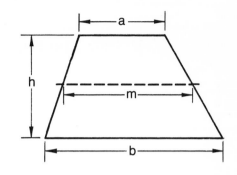

TRIANGLE

$$A = \frac{bh}{2}$$

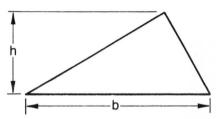

CIRCLE

$$A = \frac{d^2\pi}{4} = r^2\pi$$

$$\approx 0.785d^2$$

$$C = 2r\pi = d\pi$$

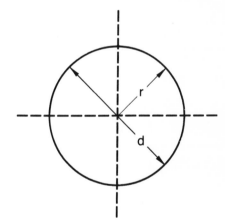

SEGMENT OF CIRCLE

$$s = 2r \sin \frac{\Theta}{2}$$

$$A = \frac{h}{6s}(3h^2+4s^2) = \frac{r^2}{2}(\Theta-\sin\Theta)$$

$$r = \frac{h}{2} + \frac{s^2}{8h}$$

$$h = r(1-\cos\frac{\Theta}{2}) = \frac{s}{2}\tan\frac{\Theta}{4}$$

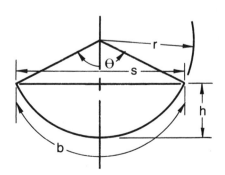

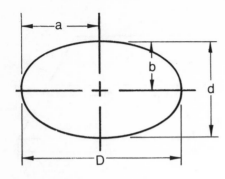

ELLIPSE

$$A = \frac{Dd\pi}{4} = ab\pi$$

$$C = \frac{D+d}{2}\pi$$

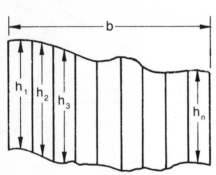

IRREGULAR SHAPE;
divide length into parallel strips
of equal width

$$A = b\ \frac{h_1+h_2+h_3+\ldots h_n}{n}(approx)$$

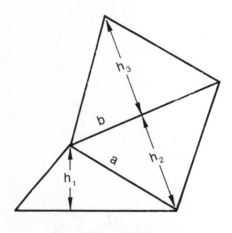

POLYGON

$$A = \frac{ah_1+bh_2+bh_3}{2}$$

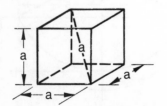

CUBE

$$V = a^3$$
$$A = 6a^2$$
$$d = a\sqrt{3}$$

CUBOID

$V = abc$
$A = 2(ab+ac+bc)$
$d = \sqrt{(a^2+b^2+c^2)}$

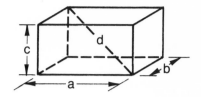

PARALLELEPIPED

$V = A_1h$

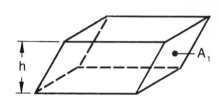

PYRAMID

$V = \dfrac{A_1h}{3}$

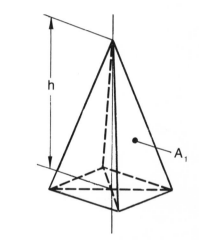

CYLINDER

$V = \dfrac{d^2\pi}{4}h = \pi r^2 h$
$A_m = 2\pi rh$
$A_o = 2\pi r(r+h)$

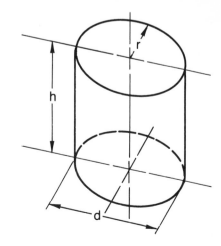

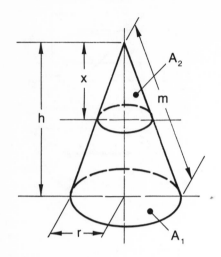

CONE

$$V = \frac{r^2\pi h}{3}$$
$$A_m = r\pi m$$
$$A_o = r\pi(r+m)$$
$$m = \sqrt{(h^2+r^2)}$$
$$A_2 : A_1 = x^2 : h^2$$

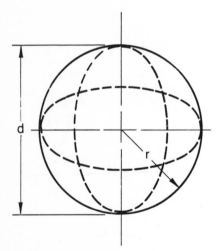

SPHERE

$$V = \frac{4}{3}r^3\pi = \frac{1}{6}d^3\pi$$
$$A_o = 4\pi r^2 = \pi d^2$$

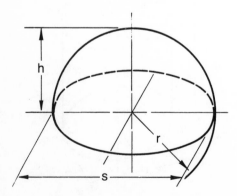

SEGMENT OF A SPHERE

$$V = \frac{\pi h}{6}\left(\frac{3}{4}s^2+h^2\right)$$
$$= \pi h^2\left(r-\frac{h}{3}\right)$$
$$A_m = 2\pi rh = \frac{\pi}{4}(s^2+4h^2)$$

BARREL

$$V = \frac{h\pi}{12}(2D^2 + d^2)$$

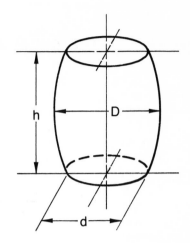

TECHNICAL ABBREVIATIONS

acfm	actual cubic feet per minute
atm	atmospheres
BS	breaking strength
BT	bottom time
cfm	cubic feet per minute
F	factor of safety
fpm	feet per minure
fsw	feet of salt water
gpm	gallons per minute
η [eta]	wave length
KSI	kilopounds per square inch
L.C.	lifting capacity
MA	mechanical advantage
NDL	no decompression limit
OVB	over bottom pressure
psi	pounds per square inch
psia	pounds per square inch absolute pressure
psig	pounds per square inch gauge pressure
Q	volume flow rate
ρ [rho]	density
Σ [sigma]	sum of
scfm	surface cubic feet per minute
SD	stop depth
SWL	safe working load

USEFUL REFERENCES

Basset, Bruce. 1977. And yet another approach to the problems of altitude diving and flying after diving! In *Proceedings of the 9th International Conference on Underwater Education*.

Bell, R.L. and Borwardt, R.E.. 1976. The theory of high-altitude corrections to the U. S. Navy standard decompression tables: the cross corrections. *Undersea Biomedical Research* 3:1-23.

Berghage, Voroxmarti, and Bernard. 1978. *An evaluation of recompression treatment tables*. Carson, CA: Best Bookbinders.

Boni, Schibli, Nussberger, and Buhlmann. 1976. Diving at diminished atmospheric pressure *Undersea Biomedical Research* 3:189-204.

Brady, Edward M. 1960. *Marine salvage operations*. Centreville, MD: Cornell Maritime Press, Inc.

Chapman, Charles. 1972. *Piloting seamanship and small boat handling*. New York: Hearst Corporation.

Cross, E. 1967. Technifacts: decompression for high altitude diving. *Skin Diver* 16(8):49; 16(2):60, 62-64, 66.

————. 1970. Technifacts: high altitude decompression. *Skin Diver* 19(11):17-18, 59.

Dietrick, Gunter. 1963. *General oceanography*. New York: John Wiley and Sons.

Edel, P. O., Carroll, J. J., Honaker, R. W. and Beckman, E. L. 1969. Interval at sea-level pressure required to prevent decompression sickness in humans who fly in commercial aircraft after diving. *Aerospace Medicine* 40:1105-1110.

Furry, Reeves and Bakman. The relationship of scuba diving to the development of aviators' decompression sickness. *Naval Medical Research Institute Research Report No. 5*.

Giles, Ronald. 1962. *Fluid mechanics and hydraulics*. New York: Schaum Publishing Company.

Guidelines for selection of marine materials. 1966. New York: International Nickel Company.

Haldane, J. S. 1922. *Respiration*. New Haven, CT: Yale University Press.

Holliday, David and Resnick, Robert. 1974. *Fundamentals of physics*. New York: John Wiley and Sons.

Harleman, Donald R. F. and Shapiro, William. 1961. The dynamics of a submerged moored sphere in oscillatory waves. *Proceedings of Seventh Conference on Coastal Engineering*, vol. 3. Richmond, CA: Council on Wave Research: University of California.

Human Underwater Biology, Inc.
   P.O. Box 5893, San Antonio, TX 78201

Ippen, A. T. 1966. *Estuary and coastline hydrodynamics*. New York: McGraw-Hill Inc.

Javier. 1978. High altitude diving tables from Mexico, *IQ 10 proceedings*. *National Association of Underwater Instructors*.

Kinsler, Lawrence E. and Frey, Austin R. 1962. *Fundamentals of acoustics*. New York: John Wiley and Sons.

Kinsman, Blair. 1965. *Wind waves*. Englewood Cliffs, NJ: Prentice-Hall Inc.

Lamb, Horace. 1932. *Hydrodynamics*. New York: Dover Publications.

Morse, Philip M. and Ingard, K. U. 1968. *Theoretical acoustics*. New York: McGraw-Hill Inc.

Myers, John J., ed. 1969. *Handbook of ocean and underwater engineering*. New York: McGraw-Hill Inc.

NOAA diving manual: diving for science and technology. 1975. U. S. Department of Commerce: National Oceanic and Atmospheric Administration Manned Undersea Science and Technology Office.

PADI Training Manual. 1972. Costa Mesa, California: PADI.

Sabersky, Rolf et al. 1964. *Fluid flow: first course in fluid mechanics*. New York: Macmillan Co.

Schenck, Hilbert. 1975. Introduction to ocean engineering. New York: McGraw-Hill Inc.

Sears, Frances. 1964. *University physics*. Reading, MA: Addison-Wesley Publishing Co. Inc.

Sienko, Michell and Plane, Robert A. 1957. *Chemistry*. New York: McGraw-Hill Inc.

Smith, C. L. 1975. *Altitude procedures for the ocean diver*. NAUI Technical Publication Number Five, National Association of Underwater Instructors.

Sverdrup, H. et. al. 1942. *The oceans*. Englewood Cliffs, NJ: Prentice Hall, Inc.

Tucker, Wayne C. 1973. Bubbles in the blood. *Skin Diver* 22(10):20.

————. 1976. Buoyancy and the diver. *Skin Diver* 25(6):34.

U. S. Navy, Diving Manual. 1974. Washington D.C.: GPO.

U. S. Navy Salvors Handbook. Washington, D.C.:GPO.

Von Arx, William S. 1962. *An introduction to physical oceanography*. Reading, MA: Addison-Wesley Publishing Co. Inc.

Weast, Robert C., ed. 1970. *Handbook of chemistry and physics*. Cleveland, OH: Chemical Rubber Company.

White, Frank M. 1974. *Viscous fluid flow*. New York: McGraw-Hill Inc.

Zinkowski, Nicholas. 1971. *Commercial oil field diving*. Centreville, MD: Cornell Maritime Press, Inc.

INDEX

ABOUT THE AUTHOR

Wayne C. Tucker is a mechanical engineer and a certified deep-sea diver. He has a B. S. in mechanical engineering from Southeastern Massachusetts University and an M. S. in ocean engineering from the University of Rhode Island. He received his technical schooling in commercial, industrial, and construction diving at the Diver's Training Academy, Fort Pierce, Florida. He has taught diving courses at the University of Rhode Island and at the College of Oceaneering in Wilmington, California.

His underwater experience includes inspections of bridges, pipelines, buoys and instrumentation, cables, and dams. He has engaged in construction diving, search and recovery, and salvage, as well as in research. He operates his own consulting diving concern, and is currently a research associate with the U. S. Navy on deep submergence systems.

In addition to the present work, he is the author of a number of articles in Skin Diver, and co-author (with John M. Malatich) of Tricks of the Trade for Divers.